The Global Woman's Impact on E-Commerce

The Global Woman's Impact on E-Commerce

Confidence and Communication Clashes with Western Corporations

Chizoma C. Nosiri

HAMILTON BOOKS

Lanham • Boulder • New York • London

Published by Hamilton Books
An imprint of The Rowman & Littlefield Publishing Group, Inc.
4501 Forbes Boulevard, Suite 200, Lanham, Maryland 20706
www.rowman.com

6 Tinworth Street, London SE11 5AL, United Kingdom

British Library Cataloguing in Publication Information Available

Library of Congress Control Number: 2019936907

This work is dedicated to Anastasia Nosiri who defines what a woman of faith, courage, elegance, and confidence ought to be. She fostered my confidence and continuously believes in me. To my children who are my biggest blessings, and to the Non-Western female consumer for she is brave, bold and beautiful. Her fight is mine; her fight is yours; her fight is ours and all is possible through God.

Contents

List of Figures

Preface

A Welcome to the World
of the Global Female

Confronting obstacles of self-confidence, cultural norms, and language barriers, discontent Non-Western female consumers (NWFC) who were born, raised, and live in China, Nigeria, and India, and who do not directly express their concerns through Western online tools, are considered mute by many Westerners. As part of the group that leads the consumer world, with over $20 trillion in annual consumer spending and figures climbing as high as $28 trillion in 2014 (Silverstein and Sayre, 2009. p. 2), the NWFC's perspective, opinions, and complaints to Western corporations' computer-mediated communication tools is non-existent and untapped, for she is unheard by Westerners on the global sphere. In an online world infused by Western cultural dominance, male-driven formation, and English-led language structures, if the NWFC is discontent with a Western corporation, the elevation of conflict brings with it multiple intimidations and battles both familiar and unfamiliar to her. The obstacles she faces mounts as she struggles to be heard on her own terms during her encounters with Western corporations' computer-mediated communication (CMC) tools.

The intent of this cross-cultural study was to determine if the Western corporations' CMC complaint of a select group of NWFCs, who were born, raised, and live in China, Nigeria, and India, is affected by their self-confidence, cultural norms, or language barriers. The study also determined the factors that make Western corporations' online tools unfavorable to the select group of NWFCs when it comes to expressing their concerns as opposed to complaining and addressing conflict issues with the local native businesses in their country. In addition, the study explored the difference in her confidence level and behavior during a complaint using corporate CMC tools contrasted with social media platforms (i.e. Facebook or Twitter). The strength of this study rests on the official qualitative research indicating the relationship and influence of self-confidence, cultural norms, or language structure of the selected group of NWFC population.

Chapter One

Introduction

The role love and belonging play in our lives is one that creates the path for our confidence and self-actualization (Maslow 1987). The need to be loved and to belong alerts us to whom we can trust during our interactions, and where we can call home. Home is where the heart is and the heart yearns for a home. Such a structure of home is an environment, a world (Lugones 1987) that fills us with feelings of acceptance, value, and ease. Although the environments we encounter may not be flawless, in the virtual consumer complaint world, the lack of belonging for a consumer who is unfamiliar with the environment is not just wrapped in complaint behavior, when confronted by conflict, but by disconfirming language structure and cultural mannerisms that diminish even the basic needs of survival within the new environment. Unfortunately, the captivating illusion of the virtual consumer world is structured and portrayed by corporations as an alluring welcoming environment (Li & Bernoff 2011), and a free world for all. However, whether the Non-Western consumer is treated as a family member, friend, guest, visitor or stranger, making a complaint is an important component to the corporation's global success (Gilpin, 2018).

The irritations of getting unsatisfying service, (with Western corporations whose products are sold strictly online), perhaps it was another Amazon.com order that was never delivered to a residence in New Delhi, India, an uncertain TransUnion error made on the credit of an individual in Hong Kong (See Appendix A), or a lack of action by Citibank to refund a Nigerian customer's account (Consumer Affairs 2014), receiving incompetent management feedback or the corporate's reluctance to resolve minor customers' issues are unlimited in the United States and even greatly unconstrained in the global environment. These consumer conflicts elevated to the global environment become massive, and are destructive to the global consumer domain structure, the Non-Western online engagement behavior, and the corporate brand on a global level. Such Non-Western consumer and corporate conflict interactions can create a catastrophe of cultural wars and clashes (Fukuyama 1999; Albirini 2008).

There are many difficult components of the situation for the Non-Western consumer to address such as distrust of the global environment, passion and energy to self-express, tension of cultural values and norms are questioned, regret of global purchase are ignited, one or all of these components may be collapsing on the Non-Western consumer. No matter the circumstances of the complaint, the situation, or the issue that promoted dissatisfaction for the Non-Western consumer, her assumed responsibility to complain to Western corporations is seen as conflictual. In the eyes of the Non-Western individual, it is not just conflictual but a conflictual circumstance that requires significant long distant interpersonal communication, a significant dependency on the unfamiliar environment of computer-mediated communication (CMC), and potentially a great amount of patience and confidence to initiate a cross-cultural communication complaint.

Online global corporate complaints that remain unresolved create disharmony between the Non-Western and Western communicators but also form online global consumer "wars" within the global environment (Consumer Affairs 2014). In addition, such global conflict exposes the Internet dynamics of the online domain and its restrictive "home" structure (between those who are familiar users "family members" versus unfamiliar users "strangers") with the procedures and process of Western consumerism and domination. Once again, the introduction of the home concept is visible. The opposition and disharmony between the Non-Western consumers and the Western corporation, its staff, management or as an entity is exposed to the flaws of the global domain structure; welcoming the Non-Western new comers and converting them to family or keeping them as strangers. This step to fight for their rights to self-express and demand for better service is approached differently by Non-Western females. The step of defending their position is one that many Non-Western females can attest to as leaving their local familiar war zone and entering into a global and unfamiliar war zone. This for them is fighting a greater war than before.

BACKGROUND

Imagine yourself as a Non-western consumer who placed an order for an item on an online Western corporate domain. During the transaction or after, you realize that you did not receive the discount the company promoted or you are dissatisfied with the product upon its late arrival. A sense of mistreatment, disrespect, or distrust may have been imposed; whether you felt unimportant, irrelevant, or simply that certain regulations of the corporation needed to be corrected. Complaining to the corporation may seem to be the easy action to take, however, the cultural obstacles, language constraints and the unfamiliarity with the global domain sparks a halt in your action. Affected by the diverse communicative restrictions and hindering dynamics of a new environment, the ability for the consumer to express concern or complaint online leaves a state of hopefulness (a positive outcome to arise) or helplessness (no possibility of resolution or improvement). In many cases helplessness because of cultural difference or language barriers is the outcome for the Non-Western female consumer (NWFC).

Generally, low self-confidence (self-efficacy) in complaint conflict for females is mainly caused by such issues as female disadvantages (i.e. leadership roles, socially structured as weak, helpless, and inferior) (Ward 2008), not being heard/understood (McKenzie-Mohr 2011), negative past experience (Parkes 1988; D'Argembeau and Van Der Linden 2008), shyness/timid nature, conflict avoidance (Wilmot and Hocker 2007), and negative past experiences to the male driven language structure (fix it mentality) that traps the female and limits the female's power to speak freely with confidence. However, these struggles for the NWFC, who is born, raised, lives in a Non-Western country, is minimal compared to the perplexed difficulties and online domain clashes that she encounters. The greater battles both in her country (local domain) and the online domain plague her, which creates a greater chance for her to become seen by Western observers and philosophers as a mute individual on the local domain and even more mute on the online domain. To expose the obstacles that create an online war zone for the NWFC and to investigate the outcomes of the NWFC confidence level in the virtual domain, an examination of the NWFC's local native business in-person complaint communication versus the CMC compliant consumer support and help venues of Western corporations becomes a necessary study.

Clearly, the great adaptation both the Western female and the Non-Western female have to endure is one that they encounter as they grow and enter into the physical domain. However, for the Non-Western female, her physical environment is one where she is not just continuously fighting to fit in as an intelligent equal contributor (Pearce, 1999; Ezumah; 2008) but literally fighting to physically exist locally and cross-culturally (Hartman 2008; Zimmermann 2014). She is faced with cultural structures that create the genocide of girls and the extermination of a gender group, as evident today in countries like India and China where more girls are eliminated yearly than the number of girls born in America every year (Davis 2012). As expressed by Evan Davis's

2012 documentary, "The three deadliest words in the world are, 'It's a Girl.'" These words remain to be words that have kept the Non-Western female unheard in her local home domain and seen as mute (Ardener 1975) by Western cultural norms. Such terror exists in every part of the world, and the fight to be seen as valued, not to be just seen, but also heard, has lasting impact on the Non-Western female's self-confidence. A diminishing confidence is presented to the Non-Western female as an individual on the first day of existence. While in some countries like China the female fights to exist (Davis 2012) because she was born a female, others like the 250 Nigerian schoolgirls kidnapped by the terrorist group Boko Haram (Bandow 2014; Embassy 2014) fight not to be used as weapons of war, while females in Indian fight against being gang-raped, killed and hanged from a tree (Tomlinson 2014). The Non-Western female is constantly fighting.

Other difficulties in cultural structure and local life control the Non-Western female and may lower her confidence. One such situation is expressed in Judith Greenberg's 2002 article "Criminalizing dowry deaths: The Indian experience." Greenberg discusses Indian women's difficulties in marriage life. After an Indian woman marries, her economic status makes leaving her new family difficult. Her dependency on her new family and being held captive in her new husband's home presents self-confidence issues in her ability to leave. Greenberg asserts that:

> Divorce, although legal is not an option. In 1991, the divorce rate was 0.3 percent. Women who leave their husbands' homes are often forced by social pressures to return. For example, the well-known feminist Flavia Agnes tells the story of Prema, who fled from her husband's home to live with a friend. Immediately, the walls of the factory where she worked were covered with signs saying that she was a slut who had run off with another man. Prema was forced to work alone and spent most of her time crying. She did not even try to get a divorce. By the end of two years, the social pressure was so great that she returned to her husband. Not only was her life miserable, but her daughter was approaching her early teens and Prema knew she would not be able to find a husband for the child if she herself remained separated from her own husband (Greenberg 2002, p.38).

The introduction of the free Western world through the global sphere virtually brought the Non-Western female a new life. With the Western mentality and the power to express streaming through the online domain, a land of the free, it gives hope to all Non-Westerners, particularly the Non-Western female (Losh, Coleman, and Amel 2013). In the 2012 article "The Role of Women in the Egyptian 25th January Revolution," Manal al-Natourher examines women's roles in the January 25th Revolution in

Egypt. She examines the representation of women's roles in digital media, specifically blogs, Facebook, and Twitter. She argues that digital social media engages women politically and provides a wide range of roles for female participation in the revolution.

Recently, many female movements have come to global attention because of the free and open platform the online domain offers. Such movements like the Me-Too movement (or #MeToo movement) is a great example of the power of the online world to unite women of all backgrounds for one cause (Kearl, 2018). The #MeToo spread virtually in October 2017 as a hashtag used on social media in an attempt to demonstrate the widespread prevalence of sexual assault, rape and harassment (Smartt, 2017). Through the structure of the online domain the Non-Western female also feels an empowerment and confidence to speak and be heard by the world. The online platform gives an amplifier like no other to the Non-Western female, to voice her opinion and also promote her confidence not only to be seen but to act, and most importantly be recognized. For example, in Saifuddin Ahmed and Jaidka Kokil's 2013 research "Protests against #delhigangrape on Twitter: Analyzing India's Arab Spring," they identified major Twitter players during the outrage against the brutal rape of a 23-year old female student in New Delhi, the capital city of India. The Twitter accounts @sakshikumar and @zenacostawrites belonged to two women who were influential in leading the movement. In addition, @sakshikumar's account was the most mentioned during the social movement protest. Ahmed and Jaidka state:

> We found that @sakshikumar and @zenacostawrites played a major role as an information source with the highest individual tweets, and they were mentioned frequently on Twitter during this social movement. Sakshi Kumar (@sakshikumar) and Zena Costa (@zenacostawrites) are core members of Justice for Women "an online movement to provide people across India a platform to marshal their resources and stand up for women who have been wronged." They started an online movement on Twitter in July 2012 as a form of protest against the molestation and manhandling of a teenage girl by a crowd of approximately 40 men outside a bar in Guwahati (Chakrabarti & Shanmugam, 2013). Both Sakshi Kumar and Zena Costa were highly instrumental in leading the protests (Ishizuka 2013; Ahmed and Jaidka 2013).

This confidence to express the dilemmas and social issues with the local domain through the virtual domain social media venues prompts a global response. In general, the global listeners who are quick to respond are Westerners. The power of social media promotes this outlet and gives the Non-Western female freedom to express her concerns. The confidence she gains from it is immense. Since the Non-Western female's approach and behavior stems from her psychological interpretation of her environment (Fromm and Funk 2013), the world she lives in, her domain, local or global, language, culture, and confidence level in expressing her concerns might differ dramatically as she runs away from her local world to the online world.

PROBLEM STATEMENT

Running away from the local world and expecting to be freed in the virtual world presents dilemmas unbeknownst to the Non-Western female. The overshadowing dilemma is whether the Non-Western female will also run from the virtual world through her consumer complaint behavior. Will she remain unheard in a virtual world created by the West? Will the Non-Western female virtual dissatisfaction prompt her to avoid expressing her concerns, and remain indifferent and powerless to the dissatisfying Western corporation online? Or will the Non-Western female voice her opinion online using other methods?

As the Non-Western female seeks rescue online through venues like social media, blogs and many other online platforms (Ahmed and Jaidka, 2013; al-Natourher 2012) she is bombarded by the Western online domain's culture (Joo 1999; Wei and Kolko 2005; McPhail 2010). Although other developing countries are working to promote their cultures online, the Western culture is one that dominates. The web-sphere was created by the West, for the interest of the West (Bickerstaff 1999; Biggs 2000), and structured in a male platform (Dholakia, Dholakia, and Kshetri 2004). In addition, the creation of this domain is associated with one major Western interest, which is consumerism (Warschauer 2000; DeVito 2010; Merriam-Webster 2014). Anything else that follows is an afterthought to propel its usage (Bickerstaff 1999).

This domain created by the West to primarily integrate economics and technology to promote Western consumerism worldwide (DeVito 2010) especially by free trade, free flow of capital, and the tapping of cheaper foreign labor markets (Merriam-Webster 2014) is covered by attractiveness of the Western ideology of beauty, power, and material goods for which the Western world wants females to desire (Colgan 2010) and consume. Ironically, although the Non-Western female may believe in the power of the Western structure to call attention to her local problems, she is unaware and does not realize the cultural structure taking over, one that eliminates her local "healthy" culture and seeps in a Western consumerism culture with an individualistic approach (Fukuyama 1999). Individualism is the basis for Western modernization. Kevin MacDonald (2010) illustrates the cultural differences among countries. His research focused on genetic differences between individualist and collectivist societies, and linked this dimension to economic growth and innovation.

MacDonald discussed that, the research for genetic marker for collectivism is the receptor gene that leads to higher stress in case of social rejection. It is clear that the individualistic and collectivistic cultures are dramatically visible between the Western and Non-Western countries. Quite clearly, individualism is a European phenomenon. The United States and other countries such as United Kingdom of Great Britain are individualistic with focus on modernization, while Non-Western countries like China, Nigeria, and India are considered collectivistic cultures which can create a divide in cultural expression approaches and a lack of belonging on the online world for the Non-Western female, diminishing her voice in expressing her concern to Western corporations online.

Without a clear understanding of the true role of the Internet, the Non-Western female can be easily trapped by the allure of the online domain's welcoming mat to a home focused on Western structure and consumerism. With every online click, the Non-Western female steps closer to accepting Western ideologies, culture mentality, and consumeristic structure of the Western world. She fully accepts a role as an online consumer, and morphs into an online Non-Western female consumer (NWFC). The NWFC openness to the online domain gives way for her to partake of the Western cultural structure and indeed consume and dwell in materialistic pursuits (Colgan 2010).

Although some NWFC are able to express their local concerns in the online domain, they open the door for the same consumer obstacles (i.e. lack of Western corporation's empathy for the consumer) that face some Western female consumers (Cluff 2012). However, the NWFC encounters more in the online domain than the Western female consumer. Even in the struggles of the Non-Western female's local obstacle, many of the obstacles have a connection to the Western ideologies consumerism and cultural pursuits. Greenberg explains this concept of the Western world's impact on dowry violence. Greenberg's point is not to attribute blame for dowry violence to family members or absolve others of the blame. She believes that colonialism, Western consumerism, and the mother-in-law, all bear some responsibility for the dowry practices and violence of modern India (Greenberg 2002).

The online domain Western consumeristic welcoming mat is laid out for the NWFC. For the NWFC, the virtual environment features all new power structures that may leave her completely powerless (Silva 2000; Kapoor 2002). Once again, the NWFC tries to fit in within a domain, a world; however, fitting in to the virtual world dominated by the Western structure may be undoable and may create an intimidation induced by fear of Western unfamiliarity.

MAJOR CONCERNS

As the NWFC steps into the online domain Western culture that she is unfamiliar with, she becomes vulnerable and dependent which may leave her unconfident (Li and Kirkup 2007). She becomes dependent on the online creators who are mainly Western operators, users, owners to guide her to perform and act as they direct her. She will remain incapable and foreign to an infrastructure that labels her incapable by design. This creates dependence on the Western system. It fosters an inferior/superior structure, a dominating structure (Freud 1993; Braidotti 1994; Kovel 2007) above those who are Non-Western within the online space. In addition, it creates a dependency on Western training system structures to provide training in Non-Western countries which promotes Western interest of consumerism and individualistic approach during training. Furthermore, the language binding obstacles such as familiarity with the English language can deteriorate the NWFC from expression and increase intimidation. The intimidation by this realization of the battle can also lower confidence to speak in conflict circumstances as she strives to accustom herself to another male dominated world (Ardener 1975).

In addition to the obstacles that plague the NWFC which may lower her confidence in complaining to Western corporations online, she faces gender related obstacles. The research conducted on gender and complaint to corporations from clients concluded that women are less likely to complain and less confidence in complaining to corporations. The lowering of confidence to express may also come from gender related issues which may foster lack of expression variables (Li and Kirkup 2007).

With all the obstacles the NWFC faces, confidence, cultural structure, and the English language are the three critical variables linked to the NWFC's ability to express complaints on Western corporations' online CMC tools. Will the NWFC revert to indirect expression, conflict avoidance, and negative word-of-mouth or will she express herself to Western corporations online? The lack of voice for the NWFC to express her concern to the conflictual party can bring with it feelings of inadequacy, inferiority, uselessness, and anger (Bradbury-Jones, Sambrook, and Irvine 2007). With such emotions, the female consumer favors instead to take a passive-aggressive role (Kelly 2006). She may decide to take action (i.e. negative word-of-mouth) or no action.

The NWFC who is an online Western shopper is not recognized (she is assumed "mute" by many Westerners) and the group size of NWFCs is also unknown (Richins 2009). Of all the studies conducted on Non-Western females and online consumerism not much attention has been devoted to the online NWFC self-confidence level and her culture as she approaches conflicting Western online circumstances in consumer purchases and complaints.

Most studies do not pay attention to the NWFC and the online Western corporation's CMC tools and its impact on the NWFC confidence or cultural upbringing. Most studies also do not explore the NWFC's online language barriers when speaking with Western personnel through their CMC tools or compare the Western corporations' online sphere to the local native business environment. In addition, not much attention has been devoted to understand the influence or impact of social media on the NWFC culture and confidence level to complain about a Western corporation.

RESEARCH QUESTIONS

This book takes a thorough look at the NWFC world through a study that answers research questions. Examining, exploring, and evaluating the NWFC perspective, view point, behavior, motives, and understanding the role confidence, culture, and language plays in her decision not to communicate directly to Western corporations' personnel in the online domain was crucial in this study, and emphasis was given to several key elements that restrict the NWFC from voicing her opinion online. Identifying the NWFC, understanding the NWFC perspective, and allowing her to express and voice her concerns, this study answered four research questions.

RQ1. Does lack of self-confidence diminish the Non-Western female consumer's voice in expressing her concerns to Western corporations through their computer-mediated communication tools?

RQ2. How do cultural differences diminish the Non-Western female consumer's voice in expressing her concerns to Western corporations through their computer-mediated communication tools?

RQ3. How do language barriers diminish the Non-Western female consumer's voice in expressing her concerns to Western corporations through their computer-mediated communication tools?

RQ4. Have social media platforms changed the Non-Western female consumer's complaint behavior and her actions in expressing her concerns through other venues?

THEORETICAL FRAMEWORK

A discourse of male-dominated and communicative structure exists online (Warschauer 2004; Joseph 2013). This discourse is one that is "prearranged" by males (Dholakia, Dholakia, and Kshetri 2004) to the point that females globally may be at a disadvantage when wishing to express matters of particular concern to them in regards to online consumer complaints and corporation dislikes. Unless the female's view is presented in a form acceptable by the dominating social culture, in many cases, the female's view is unheard and unseen (Ardener 1975, viii-ix). In addition, there is no room for women in neoliberalism (Kuruc 2008; Abdulraheem and Oladipo 2010; Fraser 2009; Al-Mahmood and Banjo 2013). As Western consumeristic structure through the online domain colonize Non-Western cultures, it brings with it the great force of Western male dominated structure of selfish individualistic pursuit with little consideration for others, particularly women who are continuously and constantly dominated.

The domination (Ardener 1975) of a low-context culture online restricts high-context cultures. Anthropologist Edward Hall presented the terms high-context culture and the contrasting low-context culture in his 1976 book Beyond Culture. When a group or community is valued over the individual, then the group favours a higher-context culture. China, Nigeria, and India are considered higher-context cultures while Western corporations are low-context culture driven (Hall 1976). These cultures rely on their common background to describe and clarify their concerns, experiences and conditions, rather than words. Higher-context cultures engage in continuing traditional ways, change little over time, and tend to promote racial diversity. They promote a close-knit community, are social and collectivist, and place a high value on interpersonal relationships (Barrett 2006; Guffey 2009).

Individuals from higher-context or low-context culture need to accommodate and adapt to the opposite culture when they engage in interpersonal communication. While not all individuals within a culture can be described by strict stereotypes of the culture they live in, it is important to understand the overall tendencies of the opposite culture which informs and educates individuals on how to better facilitate communication between individuals of differing cultures (Barrett 2006). A prominent communication characteristic of high-context cultures is that they focus more on fewer words and more on non-verbal cues, tone of voice, facial expressions, gestures, and posture. Low-context culture corporations and marketers should incorporate and utilize non-verbal communication when reaching out to high-context consumers (Solomon 2011).

Leveled by compounding matters of Non-Western structure (technology ability, culture, English language) and variations of circumstances such as in-person conflict versus computer-mediated communication (CMC) conflict, a subjected Non-Western female consumer (NWFC) does not communicate with the online Western male-dominated world, instead she digs a black hole (Ardener & Ardener 1975) of intimidation, distrust, frustration, anger, or hopelessness. She becomes overlooked and seen as invisible. She is rendered mute by Western culture. She becomes a minority (looked at by Western observers as "mute," and dominated) within a minority group (online Non-Westerner). These triple obstacles leave her as a ghost (Spivak 1988) and unheard by Western corporations. The Muted Group Theory (Ardener and Ardener 1975) is one of three theoretical structures used in this exploratory study of the NWFC. It is the overreaching theory that describes Western observers' cultural perception of the NWFC.

THE MUTED GROUP THEORY

The Western observer and the perspective of Western philosophers (Ardener and Ardener 1975; Kramarae 1981; Huston and Kramarae 1991; Wall and Gannon-Leary 1999) have framed muteness as a way to describe those who refrain from speech and are without the power of speech to express concerns, or a dominated group of individuals. However, the culture of the NWFC is one that may teach her ways to speak and express her concern without direct contact with Western corporations. These cultural tactics used by the NWFC to express her concerns are not taking into account as communicative mechanisms of expression by Western cultural standards, so a clash of cultural understanding of expression is evident. The NWFC communication and expressiveness is one structured by her culture and not one that can be classified through Western perspectives (Ardener and Ardener 1975; Alcoff 1991) as simply "mute." Therefore, muteness is not a category that can be completely applied to the NWFC group in regards to defining them as a silent group since cultural structure (Oyewumi 2002) may provide them with expressive spaces and methods that may not be observed by her culture as mute characteristics. In order to completely understand the NWFC cultural expression variables, an unsubscribing of Western ideologies of muteness is required (Spivak 1988; hooks 1990). In addition, understanding of the Western cultural domination through the online structure is necessary.

Although muteness is a Western construct and clashes with Non-Western cultures, the Western observers and philosophers' cultural understanding and framing of muteness is the same perspective of Western corporations which creates a framing of the NWFC as unheard through corporate CMC tools and viewed as a group to dominate (Joo 1999; Wei and Kolko 2005). The Western perspective of muteness has allowed Western corporations to behave in dominating ways to those they consider to be "muted." This underlining factor places the NWFC under attack as she is disregarded, unnoticed and unexpected to speak through corporate CMC tools or in other ways by corporations.

Ardener and Ardener's (1975) Muted Group Theory addressed this Western social culture flaw. Unless the female's view is presented in a form
acceptable by the dominating social culture the female's view is unheard
and unseen (Ardener and Ardener 1975). Intensified by compounding matters from Non-Western structures (i.e. technology ability, culture, English
language) which builds psychological conflict (Freud 1895), the NWFC
communication with the online Western male-dominated world is impacted,
in turn intimidation, distrust, frustration, anger, or hopelessness may set in
(Ardener and Ardener 1975). She becomes overlooked and seen as invisible
by Western corporations. She is rendered mute by Western cultural norms
and becomes a minority (considered "mute" by Westerners) within a minority
group (online Non-Westerner), within a minority (female). The Muted Group
Theory (Ardener and Ardener 1975) is one of three theoretical structures
that were used in this exploratory study of the NWFC. It is the overreaching
theory that defined the framework of the study.

The Muted Group Theory has been applied to social anthropology and
later taken up by the women's movement (Wall and Gannon-Leary 1999).
The theory has been developed most completely by Cheris Kramarae and
her colleagues (Kramarae 1981; Huston and Kramarae 1991). The theory has
been articulated primarily as a Western feminist theory to understand the perspective and perceived "muteness" of women. The theory has been applied
by Western researchers to examine subversive silences of narrative works of
Latin American women writers (Weldt-Basson 2009) and recounting wom-
en's accounts of rape or depression (McKenzie-Mohr 2011). Within the field
of communication, the Muted Group Theory has established a framework to
understand how the voices of certain cultural groups (particularly women)
are silenced by dominant group discourse (Cooke-Jackson, Orbe, Ricks, and
Crosby 2014).

To fully grasp the relevance of the NWFC's world, Muted Group theory
has been applied by Western philosophers to explain observed lack of confidence to speak up about complaints (muteness), which is assumed and
constructed by Western observers. Those who are born assertive or cultured
to speak by other venues (Oyewumi 2002) (i.e. through family members or
local community networks) may lose their voice when they enter into the
online world where they are seen as silent (mute) by Westerners, or they are
expected to be silenced and controlled by Western structures instead of in
control. Katherine Miller explains how the Muted Group theory illustrates the
muted female's position by stating that:

> Muted group theory goes beyond the concept of perception, however, and brings
> communication processes to the forefront. Specifically, muted group theory
> proposes that because the dominant group (typically white European males)

controls public means of expression (e.g., the dictionaries, the media, the law, the government), their styles of expression will be privileged. This favoring of white male communication will include everything from the dominance of rationality in public and organizational talk to the use of sports metaphors to derogatory comments and jokes about women (Miller 2005, 308).

This theory provided a conceptual model to study NWFC's cultural perspective, attitudes, intentions, subjective norms, control beliefs, and minority constraints related to specific behaviors. The NWFC low self-confidence, Western domination of culture and language within the online domain was best explored through the Muted Group Theory as the defining theory that frames the problematic online world of the NWFC since she is dominated online and may be perceived by Westerners as silent. The NWFC's decision to express her concern could be based on her discomfort. This discomfort prompts her to avoid direct contact with the Western corporation online, and instead lash out through other methods. Such discomfort and expression resolution causes her to fight several battles at once: 1) with herself (anger/disappointment); 2) cultural clash (individual versus collectivistic approach); 3) gender dominance (female stereotypes); and 4) consumer conflict (consumer/corporate war) (Ardener 1975). Within each area, the NWFC is dominated by a structure that is against her norms, gender, and ability to fight a monster created by Western minds. The NWFC is unable to express her concerns in her terms within the online complaint domain.

Shirley Ardener (1978) believed that "words which continually fall upon deaf ears may, of course, in the end become unspoken" (p.20). This is the case for the NWFC since the structure of the online domain was created to cater to males (Warschauer 2000). Males are the creators of the domain's structure and are confident in their ability to use CMC software, tools, and applications (Dholakia, Dholakia, and Kshetri 2004). The Western corporate CMC tools utilized to allow interaction and communication with the corporation are difficult for Western females to use (Cluff 2012) let alone the NWFC. The NWFC is a stranger to this structure, and moreover, she is further removed by culture and "muted" by the unfamiliar land which she has entered.

The online domain presents too many dominant individualistic models of how the society works, which prevents other groups (collectivistic approaches) to be seen as strong online cultures that should be heard (Bickerstaff 1999; McPhail 2010). Such minority groups became ignored, shut-out, and dominated. Even if the minority groups (such as the NWFC group) have a different understanding of the ways in which their culture operates (Delamont 1995), they feel subjected to being ignored because they are already considered as outsiders and "others" (Alcoff 1991; Lugones 1993; Jaggar 1998) by the West. The NWFC remains unseen if she expressed her concerns through corporate CMC online tools. This gives way to the shaping of the online society where such factors as neglect, disrespect and mistreatment influence the behavior of the NWFC. However, the molding of the global domain and the misread of the power of the NWFC group can backfire, for perceiving the group as silenced and "muted" is an error (Ardener 1975). The Muted Group Theory calls for attention to recognize the NWFC. The demand for attention to be paid to the NWFC and an understanding of the "minority" group is essential to the growth of the online domain initiatives. The NWFCs' perspective should be examined in order to determine their complaint confidence level, understand their collectivistic consumer culture, and investigate any language barriers that diminish their voice in expressing their concerns to Western corporations through corporate online tools.

Although The Muted Group Theory was the framework for the NWFC study since it profoundly describes the NWFCs as a dominated group in the online world, it must be noted that "muteness" (as Western observes would describe it) or a quietness characteristic can be an innate personality. Muteness may not be bestowed by life circumstances, culture, environmental situations (nurture) but some researchers claim that individuals may be born (naturally) quiet. It can be ingrained in an individual such as being timid, shy, or distance by birth which illustrates that a quiet approach to resolution to conflict can be infused in temperament. Looking outside Western philosophers' cultural perspective of "mute," an individual can be shy or quiet genetically (Asher 1987; Harris 2000; LeDoux 2003).

THE USES AND GRATIFICATION THEORY

The second theoretical structure that is used in this exploratory study is Katz's (1959) Uses and Gratification Theory (with particular focus on Internet usage). Initially the Uses and Gratification Theory was intended for identifying audience motivations in the consumption of radio and television media, later the theory method evolved in communications theory literature to include new media. The Uses and Gratification Theory has been applied in modern studies to cover area of information on cable transmission, video recording, TV/VCR remote control devices, as well as cellular phones as multimedia devices (Leung and Wei 2000). The theory has been employed to investigate CMC adolescents behavior (Courtois 2009), understand Internet gratification perspective (Shao 2009), and compare Facebook and Instant Messaging (Quan-Haase and Young 2010).

Since the growth of social media communication, the Internet has given way for people to express themselves and their complaints to corporations in such a manner that is not controllable by corporations. The Internet fosters, promotes, and influences online computer-mediated communication over in-person communication (McLuhan 1970). It allows consumers the ability to communicate with corporations by filing complaints and voicing their opinions through corporation online databases and tools, customer service chat boards, help desks and consumer help centers. For some, the lack of in-person interaction builds self-confidence in the consumer; therefore, they feel the right and freedom to completely speak with boldness and courage. This infrastructure and implementations of tools also gave fair playing grounds to any consumer battling with corporations, allowed the female consumer the ability, freedom, and voice of expression to complain, state opinions, and interact with the corporation without face-to-face interaction or interruption.

Recently, Uses and Gratification Theory has been updated to include gratifications sought (GS) versus gratifications obtained (GO). The GS by the audience does not always result in GO (Palmgreen, Wenner, Rosengren 1985). Social media consumer compliant conflict examples such as the "United Breaks Guitars" (Carroll 2012) viral video are ways in which consumers obtain gratification and expose corporations like United Airlines, who took the consumer's complaint seriously only after being exposed by his YouTube Video. Other social media related complaints are made popular by catch phrases like "Dell Hell" (Pang, Hassan, and Chong 2014); here the usage gratification is employed to address Dell computer problems, issues, and lack of satisfaction. The "Dell Hell" catchy phrase was created by consumers to voice their opinion on Dell products and their dissatisfactions. The use of the "Dell Hell" phrase on social media fosters a movement that promoted Dell Corporation to establish a Dell Hell support group for consumers.

The Uses and Gratification Theory places tremendous focus on the consumer, user, or spectator. Recognizing that consumers are actively involved in the online domain, the Uses and Gratification Theory is applicable to their roles in voicing their opinion. It emphasizes what individuals do with the media instead of what media does to individuals (Katz 1959). In the global sphere the social trend is that people use technology to get the things they want from corporations and each other, rather than utilizing the traditional institutional protocol or even the CMC tools of corporations. As applied to the Uses and Gratification Theory, the online sphere allows users an incredible amount of freedom to control the sphere.

As discussed in Groundswell approach, this freedom acquired by the consumers has created what is considered a "social technographic," describing categories of how consumers are gratified online as they actively use the web to control and speak about their corporate interactions. Some social technographic consumers are creators who publish blog/online articles at least once a month. Some maintain a Web page, and upload videos to YouTube. Creators are found more internationally than within the United States. For example, there are 24 percent of creators in the United States compared to 68 percent in South Korea (Groundswell 2011). Within the marketing uses, creators are opinion leaders and find online platforms to speak their minds. The conversationalists group was later added on to the Social Technographic by Forrester in 2009 because of the great use of Facebook and Twitter users (Band and Petouhoff 2009).

These users update their status at least weekly. Within the marketing uses they are actively producing word-of-mouth and are influential in networks. Then there are consumers who are critics; these individuals react to the online content of others. They post comments on blogs/online forums, ratings and reviews. Within the marketing uses they are actively producing word-of-mouth. Spectators online focus on reading and gathering information from what others produce (i.e. blogs, videos, reviews, updates). All social media users are sometimes spectators and therefore are not necessarily passive. Within marketing uses these individuals are influenced by social media (Groundswell 2011). Online users seek out ways of satisfying their needs to express their opinions and connect with others through social media platforms.

When it comes to international social technology participation, such tools like Forrester's Social Technographics data tool classifies consumers into seven overlapping levels of social technology participation, showcasing how males ages 18 through 55+ users within Metro China are actively among those who utilize the Internet as creators and critics. Forrester's Social Technographics data tool also showcases how females ages 18 through 55+ users within Metro China are actively doing likewise, even at a greater pace than their male counterparts. In addition, Forrester's Social Technographics tool gets a high-level snapshot of the social technology behaviors of metro China male consumer's online social behavior, as well as the social technology behaviors of metro China female consumer's online social behavior.

In the case of consumption and dissatisfaction, the Uses and Gratification Theory addresses the control that consumers have online as they control the online platforms. However, for the NWFC, her perspective of her power online must be examined to understand if she is familiar with the power she has to break out of being dominated (Ardener and Ardener 1975) or if she is so unfamiliar with the online domain that she remains dominated online. The Uses and Gratification Theory provides a foundation from which profiles of intended uses by consumers is constructed, which ultimately allows researchers to improve particular aspects of media for increased user satisfaction. It is considered a "how and why" approach to the understanding of media-use motivations. Gratifications are typically gathered by means of self-reported satisfaction by active users of the medium in question (Lim 2010).

Uses and Gratification Theory online users have five needs (Katz, Gurevitch, and Haas 1973; West and Turner 2010). The three most significant for the NWFC are also attached to the motivations which distinguish the role social media plays for users (Leung 2013). The first need is affective needs (i.e. emotion, pleasure, feelings), which allows the NWFC a voice to express and vent "negative feelings" about their corporate complaints and concerns. The second need is personal integrative needs (credibility, stability, and status), a "recognition" to belong and not feel disassociated and unwelcomed. The third need is social integrative needs (i.e. e-mail, instant messaging, chat rooms, and social media) which may give the NWFC the ability to connect socially and create a safe haven for growth and group of accepting friends on CMC platforms.

These are the essential needs that motivate the NWFC to express her concerns to the corporation online. The NWFC group seeks to effectively find emotional release (her voice) and status (value, courage, confidence, and empowerment). Although the negative imposition to the Uses and Gratification Theory is that the consumer has no control over what the Internet will produce in return (i.e. feedback) since there is no surety that the NWFC's voice will actually be heard through the direct corporation's online venues, yet the online social media process of expressing her concerns may empower and gratify the NWFC.

MASLOW'S HIERARCHY OF NEEDS THEORY: APPLIED TO VIRTUAL EXISTENCE

These three Uses and Gratification Theory needs: personal integrative needs; affective needs; and social integrative needs are also reflective of Maslow's Hierarchy of Needs Theory in formulation of an online world. The four most fundamental and basic Maslow's Hierarchy of Needs (physiological needs, safety needs, love and belonging, and esteem) contain what Maslow called "deficiency needs" or "d-needs." If these "deficiency needs" are not solved, the individual will feel anxious within her surroundings. For the NWFC this results in uneasiness and nervousness. Such emotional sense can produce low-confidence in task performance (Kanter 2005) or push her away from the online environment.

Maslow's Hierarchy of Needs Theory is the third theoretical structure that was used in this exploratory study. Maslow asserts that the most basic level of needs must be met before the individual strongly desires (or focus motivation upon) the secondary or higher level needs. Coining the term metamotivation to describe the motivation of people who go beyond the scope of the basic needs and strive for constant betterment (Land 2014), in the framework of Maslow's theory, the NWFC's basic needs must be met in order for her to be confident enough to gain the motivation to voice her opinion within the new online world she has entered. Instead, if she is unable to find needs that promote a "healthy" self, she will find herself dependent on the Western host (creators) for survival, indicative of Maslow's Hierarchy of Needs physiological needs and safety needs. Although we as humans are dependent on one another (Lugones 1987), if the NWFC is not allowed the ability to grow and voice her needs and wants because of the lack of completeness to function due to dependency on others to assist her on the web sphere technically or culturally (i.e., language/collectivistic approach) she will not feel that she belongs. This references the stage of "love/belonging" and not feeling "esteem," in turn confidence cannot be promoted and the NWFC's voice will remain diminished and unheard in Western CMC corporate complaints platforms.

In many instances, Maslow's theory is transferable to the virtual world (i.e. breathing, food, security, and other fundamental needs are equivalent to getting online). In the global sphere, the battle for the NWFC's to either thrive or in many cases survive is crucial to the journey she takes and how confidently she interprets herself and her abilities. As eloquently stated by Kevin Lim in his 2010 dissertation focused on the Internet control and anti-control in networked media on civil sovereignty in China, the connection of Maslow's Hierarch of Needs and the online sphere is efficiently adaptable to clarify the goals and needs of the online community users. The need for Chinese citizens to participate in online communities could also be understood in terms of Maslow's Hierarchy of Needs, where people are motivated by the urge to satisfy needs ranging from basic survival to self-fulfillment, and that they cannot fill the higher-level needs until the lower-level ones are satisfied.

SCOPE OF STUDY

The purpose of this study is to examine the Non-Western female consumer's complaint behavior strategies with Western corporations computer-mediated communication (CMC) tools online and her word-of-mouth behavior on online social platforms in relation to her self-confidence, cultural influence, and language barriers. Focus is on analyzing and interpreting the Non-Western female consumer's lack of ability to express her concerns to Western corporation personnel online. The Non-Western female consumer's dissatisfaction with the corporation's service, management, or/and products was included to examine her approach to disengage and distance herself from the corporation. Her communication in general through Western corporations' CMC tools as well as in-person local native businesses was evaluated. Clearly, Western corporations are established on local level however the true spectrum of evaluation for self-confidence changes that affect the Non-Western female consumer's behavior must be based on interactions with local native business personnel versus Western online corporation personnel.

Confidence elements and cause of lack of confidence was explored, but was limited to:

1. Confidence Level (self-efficacy and ability)
2. Unfamiliarity: Feeling of Anxiety Online
3. Cultural Clash: Western Culture Domination
4. The English Language Domination
5. Dependency on Western System/Being Seen as the "Other"
6. Historically Locally and Globally Not Being Heard/Understood

There are possible factors outside self-confidence, constructed NWFC's native land cultural norms and language barriers that may impose reasons for the Non-Western femaleconsumer (NWFC) not to express her concerns to Western corporations. Although other factors of restriction may deter the NWFC from expressing her concerns through Western corporations' CMC tools, those other factors were not addressed in this study, but were recorded if noted by a NWFC during the interview process.

The scope of this study also covered examination of the local native businesses (not including local Western corporations with local native business personnel) in-person personnel interactions. Examination of the NWFC's perspectives on utilizing online social media tools to express her concerns about the Western corporations was inquired about to find out the avenues by which the NWFC expresses her concerns online outside of corporate CMC tools. Examination of the NWFC's perspectives on utilizing the corporation's consumer CMC tools was limited to email, formal consumer service chat boards/rooms, complaint contact forms, online help desks/center, and other CMC and formal corporation's consumer complaint platforms.

This study used qualitative analysis to examine the NWFC complaint strategies and behavior to online Western corporations and local native businesses. The research consists of a sample group of NWFCs who have never left their local native land. In-depth interviewing was used to assess the participant's confidence level, impact of cultural norms and language barriers in expressing her concerns online to Western corporate CMC tools, local native businesses, and to social media outlets. NWFC subjects, born in the native country (China, Nigeria, and India), who have never left their local native land but shop on Western online websites, and are 18 years of age or older were interviewed for 30 minutes through CMC tools.

REASONING FOR SCOPE OF STUDY

The scope of this study covered the native NWFC who was born, raised, and lives in three Non-Western countries with collectivistic cultural approaches: China, Nigeria, and India. The selection of the three main Non-Western countries was geared towards their cultural approaches, significant CMC resources within the country, usage of CMC tools, and economic states of the countries.

Although Japan has the highest penetration of users on the online domain, Japan is individualistic in culture. China, on the other hand, is a collectivistic culture. In fact, the urgency to protect the culture has created sensor and monitoring of usage of the Internet with the country, however, many online users find ways to bypass sensors (Lim 2010). China is one of the world's fastest-growing economies. As of 2018, China is the world's largest economy by both purchasing power parity and nominal total gross domestic product (GDP), which makes it an ideal country to study the NWFC.

India has a population of 1.24 billion with 66 million social media users. Rivaling China in terms of potential Internet user population, India's Internet community is considered the fifth largest in the world with 60 million users, who actually account for only 5.2 percent of the country's population (Ahmed and Jaidka 2013). More recently, about 3.13 million users in India have broadband Internet connections. About 71 percent of the population lives in the rural area, where it is difficult to get Internet access, prompting a stark case of digital divide in India. However, about 14 percent of Internet users in India are bloggers (Ahmed and Jaidka 2013) and with major news being broadcast by Internet users through social media, such as the brutal rape of a 23-year old female student in New Delhi, the country witnessed a new unifying force which swept through the nation; the new force to reckon with, social media (Aiyar 2012). The world's third-largest purchasing power parity is Indian. India is the tenth-largest economy by nominal GDP, with a materialistic Western consumer drive. Notwithstanding, India is still a collectivistic country (Way and Lieberman 2010) and an ideal country to study the NWFC.

After a "rebase" Nigeria's gross domestic product (GDP) on Sunday 6 April 2014, pushed Nigeria above South Africa as the continent's biggest economy. As the richest country in Africa, and the most populous country with Ethiopia following second (Solagberu, Balogun, Mustafa, Ibrahim,

Oludara, Ajani, and Osuoji 2014), Nigeria is beginning to also be noticed on the Internet domain and the users are social media savvy. The initiation of the Nigerian Internet market is changing the picture of the online domain, as the national telecom operator (Nitel) has big plans to provide Internet countrywide. Nigeria contains a fifth of the continent's population but has been one of the slumbering giants of the African Internet world (Jensen 2000), however, it is gaining stamina in the online domain and beginning to flourish.

Although South Africa has the most Internet users in Africa, it has also been exposed to a greater extent to western individualistic values and culture (Pflug 2009). South Africans display a mixture of collectivistic attitudes (such as an emphasis on interpersonal harmony) and individualistic traits (such as materialism and an unequivocal belief in the benefits of need satisfaction) (Eaton and Louw 2000). Unlike, South Africa, Nigeria is still collectivistic, even with Western goods and supplies being imported to the country. These variables make Nigeria an ideal country to study the NWFC.

PURPOSE OF STUDY

The study reported here investigates how the Internet has transported the Non-Western female consumer (NWFC) from her well accustomed environment to a territory unknown to her. The globalization of consumerism and the increase from local to global sphere ignites the dominating Western male online sphere. The connection of the Western online domain and the desire to express her concerns when unsatisfied with Western products and services may pose cultural clashes, expose language barriers or lower the confidence of the NWFC in her complaint strategies, stripping her of her voice and rendering her silent to Western observers and Western corporations.

Although the online domain lays out a welcoming mat for all to join, the structure of the online sphere domain is catered primary to the language of the Western world which makes it problematic for the global community to feel as if they belong in the online world. For the NWFC, her battle is twice as difficult, for she fights to belong as a woman in a male constructed world and also to belong in a world created by individualistic culture. The NWFC finds herself not even a guest in the Internet domain but, a stranger to the domain. While she fights to fit, she engages in the main interest for which the Internet was created for the public, consuming Western products and slowly developing a Western mindset of materialism but never finding a home within the sphere.

While she is already trapped by other cultural male confinement locally, as enticing as it seems to enter into the global domain, which promises "freeing" variables, the chains the online domain holds for the NWFC removes her from her culture and further silences her. In order to give voice and accommodate the NWFCs, who globally controls over $20 trillion in annual consumer spending, this study's investigation focused on fully understanding the NWFC's path to living in a Western male dominated online global sphere.

SIGNIFICANCE OF STUDY

Income and labor statistics show that women globally are working and earning more than men (Catalyst 2013). Non-Western female consumers control a large portion of the world economy, and for this reason it is important on the global domain level that every effort should be made to gain the trust and loyalty of Non-Western females, as well as build the Non-Western female consumer (NWFC) online confidence. Western corporations' reputations and survival online and global sales may depend on the NWFCs' actions and other groups like them. Silverstein and Sayre (2009) proclaim the economic control women have on the global level by stating that:

> Women now drive the world economy. Globally, they control about $20 trillion in annual consumer spending, and that figure could climb as high as $28 trillion in the next five years. Their $13 trillion in total yearly earnings could reach $18 trillion in the same period. In aggregate, women represent a growth market bigger than China and India combined more than twice as big, in fact (Silverstein and Sayre 2009, 2).

Consumership power is not the only substantial power that the NWFC holds. In particular, the word-of-mouth approach (Richins, 2009) she possesses through social media and other online platforms can jeopardize corporations and their brands (Carroll 2012). The NWFC's power to pursue other venues of communication outside of the corporate CMC tools due to dissatisfaction can hinder a corporation to the point of destroying the corporation's future. The NWFC's grudge can spread through word-of-mouth (Richins 2009) circulated by web blogs and social media sites (Kline 2005). If she pursues this venue to express her concerns, not only would the corporation lose a valuable and loyal consumer, but it will also lose other loyal consumers, and if the NWFC has access to a large social media followers, that can create a corporate brand crises that may cause thousands of dollars to fix, if fixable (Carroll 2012).

Corporations who ignore the NWFC's feedback or insights on services or dissatisfactions harm their own growth and creative expansion, which limits one of the corporation's innovation avenues (Groundswell 2011). Furthermore, this research is of great value since it provides key understanding of the NWFC's cultural perspective, expectations, motives and actions. It amplifies the voice of the NWFC, allows for a change in discourse of her global position in consumerism, and empowers her. It enlightens and provides Western corporations valuable insights on proper avenues to communicate cross-culturally with the NWFC and gain the loyalty of the NWFC. The study provides Western corporations effective ways to implement strategies that will give comfort, support, and venues of expression to the NWFC.

The study gives both Western corporations and NWFCs' local businesses insight on proper communicative manners in addressing and interacting with the NWFC and particularly, customizing approaches to assist the NWFC. Moreover, this study provides social media creators and corporations insight to the influence of social media in the life of the NWFC. Furthermore, it helps Western corporations to determine ways to revamp their CMC tools, customize their online personnel approach to communicate cross-culturally with the international consumer and collectivistic customer service strategies to enhance customer satisfaction and loyalty. Generally, this study guides Western corporations on protocols in dealing with their NWFCs. Furthermore, innovative methods and CMC tools to renovate corporate "international culture" can be implemented to embrace, serve, and address the NWFC's concerns and other female consumers who in the future may be a part of the NWFC group.

Chapter Two

Literature Review

INTRODUCTION

Domination takes on various forms. No matter the target, when one entity dominates another entity the impact is long lasting and devastating. Domination is to have supremacy or preeminence over another, exercise of mastery or ruling power, and exercise of preponderant, governing, or controlling influence (Gramsci, 1996, DeVito, 2010; Machin, & Mayr, 2012; Liu-Rosenbaum, 2018). Examples of the act of "domination" listed in the Merriam-Webster (2014) dictionary leads with the Spanish domination of the Americas in the sixteenth century. Although the first known use of domination was in the fourteenth century (Merriam-Webster, 2014) domination has only increased throughout the decades and the power of those who capture and destroy increased. Domination destroys cultures, values, and traditions. Domination over an individual can destroy the individual's self-esteem, confidence; crippling the individual and consequently can hinder one's progress and life.

In the case of the "global village" (McLuhan, 1960), domination takes on different forms of colonization. Although the web-sphere can connect the world, local to the global, it can separate the world through digital divide, create a dominating environment that can capture individuals and communities, and smother cultures. This web domain, promoted by such discourses as free-net and free-market holds the keys to enter new horizons and chains to imprison new victims. In order to examine, explore, and evaluate the impact of the dominating Western online sphere on the Non-Western female consumer (NWFC) complaint confidence level, understanding the constraints that globalization presents to the NWFC is important. Engaging in this effort presents a greater understanding of the NWFC challenges of communicating and expressing her concerns in a global Western male language dominated corporate web environment.

Although loss of confidence in voicing concern during dissatisfied experiences in the global environment in many cases can be primarily influenced by gender differences, the NWFC's clash with the Western male dominated structure is the primary confidence destroyer and transformative (cultural shift) element. The impact of the global environment's Western male dominated structure (Warschauer, 2000) can cast a shadow upon the NWFC, diminishing her voice and ability to complain and progress in resolving problems of consumer complaint through her cultural norms and in her own terms. The NWFC's confidence may be controlled and even derailed as she begins to lose complete confidence in her own internal world (Parkes, 1988) as she enters in an unfamiliar world, a virtual world created by Western males. In carving out the elements that propel a Western male dominated language structure which hinders the NWFC ability to show confidence to respond to the dissatisfactory corporation web domain environment, emphasis must be given to several key elements that accompany the lack of confidence to voice her opinion.

GLOBALIZATION AND WESTERN CULTURE DOMINATION OF THE INTERNET

The online world creates a domain that allows for cultivation of new cultures (Biggs, 2000). Multiple virtual civilizations, societies and ways of life can be created. This creation embodies traditions and value system that can mold the manner in which individuals operate and conduct transactions. The virtual world can create a collective environment with shared space of intellectual inputs, and different cultures engaging in educating and supporting one another. This is the space that such a global environment can produce. In the virtual world, understanding the imposed cultural structure is important for exploring how individuals communicate and operate in transactions and interpersonal communications. A culture might stand for any community that has some unifying characteristics: religious (Christian or Jew), geographical (Asian, African), temporal (baby boomers, Gen-X'ers), characterological introverted/extroverted, morning people, night people) and even transient (Biggs, 2000).

An understanding of the cultural development of the online space showcases the community that is being created. The cultural environment the Internet holds has been examined in a plethora of research in order to explore, discover, and understand the online domain world. Eszter Hargittai gives a background on the online domain in "Weaving the Western Web:

explaining differences in Internet connectivity among OECD countries." Hargittai asserts that the Internet is a world-wide network of computers, but sociologically it is also important to consider it as a network of people using computers that make vast amounts of information available to users. Given the two services that the system provided (computer-mediated communication and information retrieval), the multitude of services allowed for by the network is unprecedented (Hargittai, 1999). The Internet was first implemented in the 1960s, and was initially restricted to a small community of scientists and scholars in just a few nations. Later the key aspect of the Internet was invented in 1990 and the Web browser, was created in 1993, which made the Internet accessible to any user (Hargittai, 1999). It was this addition to the web sphere that considerably accelerated its spread both nationwide in the United States and internationally.

Steve Bickerstaff's 1999 article "Shackles on the giant: how the federal government created Microsoft, personal computers, and the Internet" discusses the explosive growth over the past thirty plus years of the use of personal computers and the Internet for communication and its significant growth in the American economy and culture. The unparalleled success of the U.S. economy has been fueled by the growing revenues and soaring stock values generated by information technology (IT) companies and increased productivity in other industries attributable to the use of information technology. Another by-product of success of the U.S. economy is the increased use of both the Internet and personal computers. Americans conduct their businesses, run their households, raise their children, search for or obtain information, conduct their political campaigns, and entertain themselves through CMC. The greatest effect has been and will increasingly be on how and what people communicate (Bickerstaff, 1999).

Several researchers have argued that the Internet offers an unprecedented opportunity for under-represented groups to showcase their aboriginal languages, cultures, and values. However, there can be few real social and cultural exchanges as long as the English culture, language and Western values dominate the Internet (Joo, 1999; Wei, & Kolko, 2005). Thomas McPhail (2010) elaborately describes the impact of the Western domination in regards to media, particularly films and news expansion and the crisis presented to European film and other media industries. United States feature films hold shares far above 50% in most markets throughout the world. In addition, United States feature films hold over 90% in the domestic American market compelling EU to pay closer attention to United States film and other media industries (McPhail, 2010). This Western media domination is a great example of how the culture of the West and the English language dominates internationally.

Other researchers believe that the size of the Internet and the nature of its users together create a demand for more complex cultures and communities in cyberspace (Jordan, 1999), typical of different cultures. Although there is a need for more complex cultures and communities, many express differences and claim that the Internet "is also an experiment with the basic symbolic and moral foundations of mainstream Western culture and how these foundations are inter-generationally renewed" (Bowers, 1998, p. 112). They claim that not everyone and every nation welcome globalization. For example, the globalization of the mass media for many peripheral nations and some industrialized nations such as Canada, France, and Ireland, are concerned about the dominance of US global media exports. For the United States, a central objective is to win the battle of the world's information flows, dominating the airwaves as Great Britain once ruled the seas (McPhail, 2010). This Western domination structure is fueled with such acts from foreign producers who tend to copy the news magazine or reality show format of the Western programs (i.e. MTV) and create indigenous programs with US cultural values and insert local content such as announcers and venues. Similarly, the Internet has the same effects without the control by most foreign land government authorities, which gives individuals in foreign countries access to the Internet filled with Western creators (McPhail, 2010).

As McPhail (2010) explains the Western domination structure of Western media and foreign values as applied through the World System Theory (WST). This is useful in examining cultural industries, mass media systems, audiovisual industries, technology transfer, knowledge, regulatory regimes, and activities of the biggest global stakeholders, which pursue interrelated strategies to maximize corporate growth, market share, revenues, and profits. Evidently, globally there is domination by Western culture. McPhail (2010) asserts that, "the three zones of WST reflect a world where the living standards are extremely broad. Modernization and globalization have failed to produce the economic and social change that many academics and policy experts predicted" (p. 30).

There is also a substantial and important link between the Electronic Colonialism Theory (ECT) and the WST. The ECT suggests that when exported the mass media carry with them a broad range of values. These values are social, cultural, economic, and sometimes religious or political in nature. Increasingly they carry with them the English language, in terms of pop-culture, movies, or music. Dividing the nations of the globe into three categories, the WST theory extends ECT. The WST then expands on how the core category works to influence the two subordinate categories.

Some core nations are concerned about the impact and penetration of ECT and worry about the Americanization of their domestic cultural industries and consumer behavior. Nations in the subordinate categories (semi-periphery and periphery) have a multitude of reasons to be concerned about the implications of ECT. In the semi-peripheral and peripheral zones, the consumption of media from local monopolies is frequently being replaced with Western media and foreign values that have had considerable cultural, economic, regulatory, and political repercussions over time (McPhail, 2010, p. 32).

Others believe that in most societies, resistance to cultural change is the norm, and those who share a culture cannot just plug in new values and norms and unlearn the lessons that have been taught to them over their lifetime (Houston, 2003), for the lessons are buried in their memories and in the institutions of the society. This may be a factor to the lack of cultural transformation or cultural domination of one set of cultural norms. However, as described in many culturally flexible societies, even established values and norms are by definition open to such challenges and changes by allowing innovations to be used (often via sub-cultures) in conducts that are possibly inconsistent with their foundational cultural norms and thereby, exposing groups with cultural norms to accept cultural changes and possible domination from other cultures (Houston, 2003). As stated by Francis Fukuyama (1999), the tensions and powerful influence of cultural change or domination presented by the Internet gives way to a lessened belief that, the underlying society will continue to enjoy the right sort of cultural values and norms they covet when they are under the pressures of technological, economic, and social change that the Internet houses.

On the contrary, in a study that examined Thai culture, the focus was on how the Internet brings homogenization of the local cultures to the global environment. Through an examination and explanation of a Usenet newsgroup, soc.culture.thai, it found that, instead of erasing local cultural boundaries, creating a worldwide monolithic culture, the Internet reduplicates the existing cultural boundaries (Hongladarom, 1999). The Thai culture study evidence showed that, instead of looking at the Internet as a sign of the world becoming culturally monolithic, we may have to look at it just as a global forum where participants join one another so long as there is a felt need for it (Hongladarom, 1999). Although the Thai study was engaged in exploring the ways in which culture is shared among groups in the Internet, the underlining forms of how groups operate in the global community in regards to promoting cultural components with others of the same culture in the global community, however, other studies (Bowers, 1998; Wei, & Kolko, 2005) have proven that the Internet global community is eliminating other cultural values and Western culture dominates (Fukuyama, 1999; Albirini, 2008).

While some critics are concerned about the expanded threats of Western cultural "hegemony" to indigenous cultures, other critics believe that every nation is likely going to face cultural challenges brought on by the Internet. Nations with well-developed Internet infrastructure will have far less cultural disruption, while other nations with underdeveloped Internet infrastructure will face cultural changes (Houston, 2003). On the other hand, researcher Terranova (2000) stated that the multiple cultures within the Internet domain will enrich the global economic value. She asserted that the process of cultural integration is usually considered the end of a particular cultural formation. Terranova (2000) states that, "After incorporation, local cultures are picked up and distributed globally, thus contributing to cultural hybridization or cultural imperialism (depending on whom you listen to)" (p. 38).

Alternatively, Albirini (2008) asserts that the Internet dissemination into developing countries is not just highly profitable to the computer industry but also a trial with the basic symbolic and moral foundations of Western culture. The Internet transmits the ideas and values of the Western society. These values and ideas have played a critical role in the design and development of the media. Furthermore, the Internet was not designed to be used by "peripheral" cultures and such cultures were not influential in its evolution, design or functionality (Wei & Kolko, 2005).

In contrast to the view of the Western domination of the Internet, some researchers have said that in order for individuals to function in a wired world, they will need to become more bi-culturally high on both independence and interdependence since they believe that availability of both types may be necessary to communicate and function in a multicultural environment (Yamada & Singelis, 1999) such as the Internet. On the contrary, Albirini, (2008) states that, "on a cultural level, the Internet's predominantly Western design, content, and language have facilitated the proliferation of alien cultural patterns at the expense of the social experiences of the local cultures." Even in the classrooms, the Internet is shaping cultures, deleting some and promoting others. The study done by Jae-Eun Joo (1999) portrayed how the Internet impacts cultures in schools and how educators have paid relatively little attention to the cultural impact of this new technology in teaching and learning. This study calls for an urgent need to reshape the Internet as a human, rather than merely computer network.

Ironically, Houston (2003) believes that this "human" Internet is likely to increase human tensions. He affirms, "the Internet can foster global network organizations with intimate social groups that might be exclusionary such as tribal communities; however, it will create cultural threats to the status quo because it offers so many economic, cultural, and political alternatives" (p. 354). Although repressive political regimes may be especially vulnerable to Net-induced change, other institutions such as Western democracies, religions, corporations, and cultures are at risk. This risky change that may affect even Western culture promotes all to recognize that Internet access creates chaos with cultures in many parts of the world (Houston, 2003). The argument continues as some researchers insist that the Internet promotes all cultures to be part of the playing field. India is reaching out to multiple audiences globally and has become an active player in the global media industry, shaped by the globalization of media, local, and national cultures. The fear of cultural imperialism encourages many countries of the world to create protectionist policies in order to maintain control over their indigenous cultures.

Furthermore, the growing availability of communication satellites has increased diversity of the global cultural scenario. On the other hand, Fukuyama (1999) believes that pluralism and tolerance built into the formal institutions tend to encourage cultural diversity. However, individualistic culture has the potential to reduce other cultures inherited from the past. Fukuyama's evaluation is the core center of the threat from Western culture domination of the Internet and its impact to erase other societies' cultures and values.

ENGLISH LANGUAGE GLOBAL DOMINATION

The domination of a global language is one that would cause a threat to all other languages and in some cases a threat to civilizations, for with language comes culture, values, and lifestyles (Machin & Mayr, 2012). Language creates existence (Wodak & Mayer, 2009) and through this existence is the power to cultivate the structure in which societies operate and function. A global language impact can hinder well established and developed countries and on the other hand can destroy developing countries (Machin & Mayr, 2012). However, the enormous effect is much greater than the global platform, since such domination will seep into the local language structure of less developed indigenous communities. Taking language from the global to the local jeopardizes the local society domain and penetrates cultural boundaries, creating a domination of a foreign language in local environments.

In order to understand the significance of the global domination implications of the English language, there are two fundamental components of the English language that must be addressed. The first is the English language global domination which fosters a notion of its usefulness compared to other languages (Hachten & Scotton, 2006). The second is the global domination of the individualistic tones of the English language and the relevance it infuses in communication process with societies outside of the Western, high-context and collectivistic cultures (DeVito, 2010; Beebe, & Ivy, 2012).

As asserted by Foucault (1972), "every [organization or corporation] system is a political means of maintaining or modifying the appropriation of discourse, with the knowledge and the powers it carries with it" (p. 1). The Internet's creation is a system infused with content (i.e. language mannerisms, English text, and rhetoric) by its creators (Wei & Kolko, 2005; McPhail, 2010), laid out by the creators to politically suggest their intentions, goals, and interests (Albirini, 2008). The early dominance of English language on the Internet was due to a high percentage of early users who were North Americans. The computer experts who designed private computers and the Internet did so on the basis of the American Standard Code for Information Interchange. The Internet brings together users in many countries and has furthered the need for people to communicate in an international language and strengthened the position of English language in that role (Warschauer, 2000).

The English language plays a critical role in the design and development and usage of the media (Wei & Kolko, 2005). Globalization heightens the role of English as an international language. On the contrary, others believe differently. For example, Alexander Solzhenitsyn believes that the global domain has promoted multiple languages in the printing and broadcasting industries (Hachten & Scotton, 2006). However, intentionally, the Internet and other technologies transmit the culture, ideas and values of the Eurocentric society.

Although some see the global environment as promoting multiple languages, many researchers who study applied linguistics and the English language impact on other countries see strong signs of English language domination globally. In Kata Csizer and Zoltán Dörnyei (2002) study, they examined how the significant sociocultural changes that took place in Hungary in the 1990s affected school children's language-related attitudes and language learning motivation concerning five target languages, English, German, French, Italian, and Russian. Dörnyei and Csizér's analysis were based on survey data collected from 8,593 13/14-year-old pupils on two occasions, in 1993 and 1999. Dörnyei and Csizér (2002) assert that, "an unexpected but potentially important finding was that during the examined period the learners' general language learning commitment showed a significant decline, with only English maintaining its position" (Dörnyei & Csizér, 2002, p. 421). Such a finding can be seen as a reflection of a more general 'language globalization' or the study of the world language (English) against other foreign languages.

Alternatively, many believe that the newspapers and computer-mediated communication technologies are promoting multiple languages and inclusion of all written language text. Hachten and Scotton (2006) assert that newspapers have evolved towards becoming global. Newspapers like London based Financial Times, Le Monde of Paris, and International Herald

Tribune of Paris have increased in readership, publishing in more than 60 languages. Such Western programs like the NBA finals have been brought into 109 countries in twenty languages. Millions in Europe can now watch Oprah Winfrey, subtitled or dubbed (Hachten & Scotton, 2006). Furthermore, some authors believe that the global sphere is allowing for all languages to participate voluntarily in customizing the languages. In Chapter 4 of Goldsmith and Wu's 2006 book, Who controls the Internet?: illusions of a borderless world, they stated, "English websites originally dominated the Internet, but as time progressed, the percentage of websites in English substantially decreased" (p. 7).

Unfortunately, subtitles and non-English web creators will not be enough to decrease domination of the English language. Researchers for years have been noting English as the global language even before the creation of the Internet environment infrastructure. The global environment is another domain where there is a continuation of fostering Non-Western individuals to learn and adapt to the English language. English is the media language (Hachten & Scotton, 2006). English has become the global language of science and technology. English is the most taught language in the world. Globally, English has also become the leading media language for international communication (Hachten & Scotton, 2006). Lydia Slater gives examples of comments (Warschauer, 2000; Crystal, 2001) asserted by individuals in regards to the English language global domination,"A linguistic perspective. Will the English-dominated Internet spell the end of other tongues? Quite e-vil: the mobile phone whisperers. A major risk for humanity" (Crystal, 2001, p. 1).

This quotation illustrates the generally held anxieties about the effect of the Internet on other languages. Interestingly, the first is the sub-heading of a magazine article on millennial issues. Such headlines demonstrate the difference between languages and opinions of language option. The second is the headline of an article on the rise of new forms of impoliteness in communication among people using the short messaging service on their mobile phones. These headlines assert the concerns of many about the English dominated Internet and the end of other languages. The third is a remark from the President of France, Jacques Chirac, commenting on the impact of the Internet on language, and especially on French. Slater claims that her collection of press clippings has dozens more comments that are similar to the quotes above, all with a focus on the domination of the English language (Warschauer, 2000), all expressing concerns. They are all worried about linguistic issues.

In contrast, Sherry Turkle (1995) asserts that re-localization generates space for other national and local languages to reaffirm themselves. Although some scholars continue to claim that English is not dominating other languages and that the global environment has room for all languages, many researchers assert that English is now spoken as a second language by more people around the globe by the British and the Americans combined, it must now be considered as belonging to the world (Hachten & Scotton, 2006). Albirini, (2006) illustrates the English domination facts by stating that, "In many cases, the under-representation of the local languages on the web generates negative attitudes toward the Internet and discourages many individuals in developing countries against taking advantage of the promising aspects of the medium" (p. 49). This realization of English as the global language cultivates implications of Western structures, values, and cultures which promote a silencing of other cultures, in particular, collectivistic cultures that focus on accommodation, compromise, and collaboration (DeVito, 2010; Beebe & Ivy, 2012). English language domination creates language, cultural, and gender clashes of communication differences between Western corporations and the NWFC, which diminishes her voice in expressing her concerns.

NON-WESTERN FEMALE DEPENDENCY: ADDRESSING THE "OTHER" ON THE GLOBAL SPHERE THE HELP OF THE WEST

We as humans are dependent on one another (Lugones, 1987). Whether we embrace this reality or not is our own battle. Although dependency is necessary, those whom we depend on can either assist to propel us or can diminish our ability to grow. In the case of the NWFC, there are two main reasons why dependency becomes a problem for her. First, she is unable to function completely because she does not belong and have to depend on others to assist her technically or culturally (i.e., language/collectivistic approach, stereotypes) on the web sphere.

This is similar to the stage of "love/belonging" as explained in Maslow's "Hierarchy of Needs" If one does not have this sense of dependency (Jaggar, 1998; Alcoff, 1991) and belonging, the next stages above "esteem" (confidence) and self-actualization in Maslow's "Hierarchy of Needs" are unreachable. The second dependency issue is when an individual is overly dependent on others to the degree of being unable to survive in the global sphere without the help of others. Utilizing Maslow's "Hierarchy of Needs" this would fit into the "physiological" stage or the "safety" stage. In this instance breathing, food, security, and many fundamental (which are equivalent to getting online-existing on line, and basic interactions online are non-achievable) necessities are prominent and the dependent would need assistance to receive these substance in order to survive. In the global sphere, the battle for the NWFC dependency to either thrive or in many cases survive is crucial to the journey she takes.

Many scholars and researchers have connected "dependency" of Non-Western structure to the West from a structuralist and socioeconomic perspective, seeing imperialism and development as tied to the unfolding of capitalism. Kapoor (2002) based his research on the works of Frank, Cardoso, Faletto, Said, Spivak and Bhabha. Kapoor asserts that ". . . dependency chooses a structuralist and socioeconomic perspective, seeing imperialism and development as tied to the unfolding of capitalism, whereas postcolonial theory favors a post-structuralist and cultural perspective, linking imperialism and agency to discourse and the politics of representation" (Kapoor, 2002, p. 647).

As adequately elaborated by Forrester Research executives, Charlene Li and Josh Bernoff in their book Groundswell (2011), on the global sphere, individuals and companies are taking advantage of emerging social technologies and eagerly using social technologies as creators, critics, collectors, joiners, spectators, while some remain inactive and have yet to fully experience the web world. The realization that companies are no longer able to control customers' attitudes through market research and customers are controlling the conversation by using new media to communicate about products, Groundswell teaches companies how to use social technologies strategically and effectively to gain favoritism with customers and prevent negative branding. The secondary focus of opening doors to build intercultural communication is an addition to the primary focus of the online domain. This sphere allows all participants to be involved in a constructed manner that lays out a welcoming mat for all to participate. However, at what cost are participants positioned as family, guest, or completely strangers?

Non-Western females are among the groups who are eager to enter the global sphere. The prize of being a part of this sphere is one that calls for investigation as to who is treated how and in the case of the Non-Western female, what type of welcome mat and sphere is she stepping into? Is it a sphere where she feels the "freedom" to be and exist instead of dominated (Ardener, 1975)? In order to understand the significance of the global Non-Western female's dependency, we must address her contribution, impact, and voice on the global domain to get a greater perspective of her world in the global sphere.

Many researchers assert that the global Non-Western female's world is one where she finds herself continuously depending on Western empowerment (Aderemi et al., 2008). With eagerness, the Non-Western female's goal of launching business in the web sphere is met first hand through the help of Western establishments. On the other hand, other researchers believe that the majority of Non-Western females, especially those outside of the professional environments, are not interested in entering the web domain (Joseph (2013). In contrast, Aderemi's (2008) research expressed that many of the

Non-Western female entrepreneurs (in countries like Nigeria) requested for financial assistance from the government to enable their businesses develop into significant economic contributors and participate in the global economy. Some researcher's explanation of the Non-Western female's advancement to become more familiar or accustomed to the ways of the Internet domain is structured in a manner that perceives them as lacking, unqualified and needing training in the Internet domain. On the contrary, other researchers stated that Non-Western females lack training and understanding of the online domain (Evans, 1995; Joseph, 2013). Aderemi (et al., 2008) research on Nigerian entrepreneurs asserted the need for Nigerian women to develop innovative skills and culture, network with government agencies or vice versa and develop strategic alliance among them. This would enhance competence in their respective specializations and build the global competitiveness of their firms. The Non-Western female is stepping into a domain that she is: 1) unfamiliar with-newness, vulnerable and dependent; and 2) unavailable to perform because of her lack of competence-lacking in technology understanding and experience. She is stepping into a world where she does not belong but must adjust to and is dependent on the creators who are mainly Western male online operators and users (Warschauer, 2000; Dholakia, Dholakia, & Kshetri; 2004) to guide her to perform and act as they direct her. In addition, it creates a dependency on Western training system structure to provide training, promotes Western interest of consumerism and Western culture.

Aderemi's (2008) study showed that Nigerian women's technological ventures are greatly enhanced if they "are moderate in attending to family, love and responsibility (that is, not being sentimental in business)" (p. 174) and many female entrepreneurs are inspired into starting technological businesses more on the basis of personal interest than unemployment. These two components dismiss the Non-Western female's collectivistic cultural identity and connection of family dependency and foster a Western individual mental state and dependency on Western cultural structure.

NON-WESTERN FEMALE CONFIDENCE AND ANXIETY ON THE ONLINE SPHERE UNFAMILIAR TERRITORY

Researchers have illustrated how education and national culture may influence Internet use. One particular study explored factors that might facilitate college students' use of the Internet across samples in four countries: India, Mauritius, Reunion Island (an overseas Department of France), and the United States. The results of the study suggested that Non-Western samples reported greater desire for Internet access and non-English websites. Having non-English websites would increase the chance of the online interactions. In addition, training on how to use the Internet and course requirements for Internet use were reported as helpful by the India and Mauritius groups to a greater extent than by those in Reunion and the United States (Fusilier, Durlabhji, Cucchi, & Collins, 2005).

On the other hand, another study investigated the relationships between acculturative stress of East Asian international students and their use of the Internet, taking into account Internet types (English-language Internet and native-language Internet) and Internet motives. A research which included participation from 115 East Asian international students who attended a large urban university in the southeastern United States was initiated. On the average, students used English-language Internet more than native-language Internet, suggesting that English was preferred and wanted more than native languages. Furthermore, a positive correlation was found between using English-language Internet and English proficiency (Ye, 2005). In contradiction, the issues of non-English and English usage online is a national culture issue and according to Nai Li and Gill Kirkup's, 2007 study which focused on British and Chinese students asserted the following results:

> Most British students (91%) reported that they only looked at English language websites, because most websites are English language and American dominated (89%). Most Chinese students (72%) not only looked at Chinese sites but also visited English language websites. Language sometimes caused difficulties for Chinese students using the Internet. For instance, some mentioned that they did not like using the Internet just because there were too many English language sites, and their English was not good. (Li & Kirkup, 2007, p. 311)

Although some researchers are claiming that language does create dependency that formulates lack of ease within the global sphere for those unfamiliar with English, while other researchers claim it does not create dependency for those who are not native English speakers because they prefer English more. The gender divide on the global sphere is even more contradicting. Many researchers believe that gender differences affect the level and ability of use of the Internet and also suggest that gender stereotypes are attached to the web domain. One of Li and Kirku's main objective was to investigate whether the results of previous research into gender differences in the use of the Internet, focused largely on Western residents (i.e. American, Australian and European students), was similar for Chinese students. Li and Kirkup asserted that a social constructionist viewpoint suggested that the association between gender and technology is one where, "Both gender and technology are processes; they are shaped, or acted out, in interaction" (Silva, 2000, p. 613). Li and Kirkup claimed that technology and gender change simultaneously with the cultures they are connected to and together they are socially and traditionally molded (Li & Kirkup, 2007).

Li and Kirkup's (2007) study investigated the effects of online apprehension and gender. They surveyed 608 undergraduate students (118 males and 490 females). Their study measured the students' experience with the Internet and their levels of Internet anxiety. They discovered several gender variances in participants' use of the Internet. Li and Kirkup asserted that unlike the females, males were proportionately more likely to own web pages. Males also utilized the Internet more and were more likely to use game websites than females (Li & Kirkup, 2007). In addition, males utilized the Internet for communication proposes more than females (Joiner, Gavin, Duffield, Brosnan, Crook, Durndell, & Lovatt, 2005). On the contrary, other researchers have stated that females utilize the Internet more for communication purposes more than men (Gibbs, 1998; Odell, Korgen, & Schumacher, 2000; Savicki & Kelley, 2000; Jackson, Ervin, Gardner, & Schmitt, 2001). Li and Kirkup believed their results suggest that the Internet utilization shadows computer utilization. They assert that British women look at the Internet as a tool while their male counterparts see it as a toy (i.e. gaming system or fun engaging platform). Although the Internet was originally invented in a male dominated environment, however, the Internet's use is no longer limited to men, but both computers and the Internet are still characterized as masculine. Li and Kirkup also mentioned that their finding confirmed examination of gender stereotypes about the Internet and computer usage (Li & Kirkup, 2007).

Also, the Li and Kirkup, 2007 study investigated gender differences and cross-cultural context in utilization of and approaches toward computers and the Internet for 220 Chinese and 245 British undergraduate students. The undergraduate students were between the ages of 18 and 23 years old. Their research found that, in both countries, the male students reported more recurrent usage of e-mail than their female counterparts. Although female students conveyed pleasantness in utilizing using e-mail, they used it less than their male counterparts. In analyzing Li and Kirkup's (2007) research, there is a contradiction with other research literature which suggests that women culturally are more involved in interpersonal communication activities. However, Li and Kirkup study suggested that, when communication is facilitated through a masculine technology, females become less interpersonal communicators. In the Li and Kirkup study, the female students in both Britain and China held sturdier beliefs that females have capabilities equivalent to their male counterparts in the usage of the Internet. Eighty percent of the Chinese female students agreed that their male counterparts spend more time surfing the web and using computers than they did, while Britain females did not agree. In addition, in both countries the females were less likely to be familiar with the Internet than their male counterparts. This suggests that both the Chinese and Britain females were more foreign in the online atmosphere. The male students in both countries held even sturdier negative gender stereotypes. The male students believed that Internet usage was an activity more appropriate to males. Li and Kirkup asserted that gender stereotypes about Internet and computer usage were socially accepted by both males and females in Britain and China. In the Li and Kirkup (2007) study, the female students believed that their male counterparts were more likely to use computers and the Internet more than them.

Li and Kirkup asserted that their finding showcases how males and females transfer gender stereotypes into the online sphere environment and then continuously practice gender stereotypes online. Furthermore, Li and Kirkup (2007) found significant differences in Internet experience, approaches, usage, and self-confidence. Li and Kirkup asserted that the British students were more likely to use computers for education purposes than Chinese students, however, Chinese students were more self-confident about their advanced computer skills. In both countries, the males were more likely than females to utilize chat rooms and e-mail. Both the Chinese and Britain males were more self-confident about their computer abilities and skills than their female counterparts. Li and Kirkup asserted that, "men were more self-confident about their computer skills than women, and were more likely to express their opinions that using computers was a male activity and skill than were women" (Li & Kirkup, 2007, p. 301). This understanding that computers are a male activity may disassociate the female user and places her as a stranger to the platform. It stereotypes her as unable to function equally online and diminishes her confidence in expressing herself in her own way through the online sphere. On the other hand, Durndell and Haag (2002) explained how research on gender and computing has often, although not always, produced results which indicate greater male than female experience and use of computers (Brosnan & Lee, 1998 in the UK; Balka & Smith, 2000, in the USA). There is also a tendency that females have more negative attitudes towards computers than males (Durndell & Thomson, 1997, in the UK; Whitely, 1997, in the USA), and similarly, there is an inclination of greater computer anxiety among females than males (Maurer, 1994; McIlroy, Bunting, Tierney, & Gordon, 2001). However, one of the few examples of a reverse finding was in Hong Kong, where males were more computer anxious than females (Brosnan & Lee, 1998). In contrast, Todman (2000) found that the male female gap in computer anxiety, with females being more anxious, was increasing through the 1990s in the UK, whilst McIlroy et al. (2001) found this difference to be slightly declining but persisting in the USA.

These varied findings alert for the concern for anxiety related usage issues and Internet experience that can lessen the female's confidence in the online sphere and communication competence. Further research on cross-cultural gender confidence online investigated by Li and Kirkup (2007) confirmed a lack of confidence for females cross-cultural in the global sphere. Li and Kirkup asserted that the Chinese and Britain male students who were asked about their confidence in using the Internet for numerous activities reported greater confidence, while their female counterparts were significantly reported that they 'got lost' in such activities like searching the Internet.

All the female student participants in the Li and Kirkup's study undervalued and underestimated their ability to use computers and the Internet. In information searching tasks both the Chinese and Britain females performed as well as their male counterparts. However, the female students were more likely to report finding difficulties doing the information searching tasks. Li and Kirkup's (2007) results indicated that the Chinese female students seem to attribute their own abilities to use the computer and the Internet as lower than their male counterparts. Although Li and Kirkup's research suggested that females are less confident in the online domain, Joseph's (2013) more recent research based on Canada and New Zealand females suggested that most Non-Western females who have access to the Internet generally tend to be from higher socio-economic levels, are better educated, usually employed in established professions, and tend to be young (Balka, 1995). These young females were more experienced with the Internet and had frequent assess to it. Such a situation would promote a more confident woman who already has Internet skills.

In Joseph's 2013 Canada and New Zealand study, he investigated the experience of a private-sector facilitator in developing and offering an online course through the Women's International Electronic University. The study highlighted the challenges that most Non-Western female's face in overcoming barriers to participation in continuing education. Joseph stated that social economically stable females were not at all the broad spectrum of females who were being targeted by the project. However, the sample of those females who participated for Course 003 were teachers, university professors, doctors, lawyers, computer technicians, health care workers, media personnel, or government officials. Due to the financial constraints imposed upon the provider, it was nearly impossible to reach those non-professional, lower income females for whom Web-based courses might be most valuable (Joseph, 2013, p. 54). Furthermore, researchers have found that most analysis indicates that perception and satisfaction differences exist between the cultural clusters and gender groups within those cultures-Asia, Europe, Latin and South America, and North America. In particular, the perceptions of the Asian and Latin/South American were found to be similar, as were the perceptions of the Europeans and North Americans.

This may attest to the cultural divide in collectivist and individualistic mannerism that exists between the cultures (Simon, 2000). However, using an adapted version of Hofstede's dimensions as a means of differentiation on perception and satisfaction levels on four websites, the qualitative analysis conducted by Simon (2000) indicated that females within certain cultures have widely different preferences from their male counterparts regarding website attributes. Such a result indicates the "culture" difference between males and females in regards to online preferences. There are other factors that play an important role in creating barriers for females in the online domain. Joseph (2013) asserted that, ". . . women who want to learn about technology are often overlooked in course design and development" (Joseph, 2013, p. 48) Most of these women are intimidated when learning a non-traditional skill in a mix-gendered environment, where power structures, subtle gender biases and lack of role models chip away at their self-confidence.

Although barriers exist which can lower self-confidence and create anxiety for the Non-Western female, cultural factors could influence the propensity to adopt a given technology in performing a certain function by making the "alternative technology" less or more attractive. For example, Dholakia, Dholakia, and Kshetri (2004) illustrated the attractiveness of the web to remove relationship formation barriers. The fast increase in the number of female Internet users in Saudi Arabia is driven by women's use of the Internet for personal and business reasons. Women are not allowed to drive cars in some Muslim countries such as Saudi Arabia. However, in Muslim societies, open and public interactions between men and women are highly constrained outside of marriage and family. The Internet helps overcome interaction barriers between men and women. The Internet proved to be a better alternative for women in the Middle Eastern given the restricted public intermingling of the two sexes. (Dholakia, Dholakia, & Kshetri, 2004)

In contrast, although this attractiveness exists, Dholakia, Dholakia, and Kshetri (2004) agree with many researchers that the main concern and issues that foster low confidence and create anxiety for the Non-Western female in the global domain is based more on gender difference and perception of what gender the Internet was created for. Although the gloominess of the global domain hovers over females, courses offered via the Web, which offer some unique advantages beyond those of more traditional modes for females exist. Evans (1995) asserted that when educating Non-Western students through more traditional correspondence-type courses, it is difficult for an institution to provide support to participants who may need to overcome problems such as study fear or lack of confidence. In particular, this is even more difficult for students who live in geographically isolated areas (Evans, 1995).

The world view and language interpretation between males and females are points of difference similar to those found in "intercultural" communication, and this too points to the benefits of a single-gender learning environment. On the other hand, Non-Western females believe other barriers exist that diminish their voices as participants online, such as gender socialized differences. Gender socialized differences in communication and viewpoints between men and women may contribute to the lack of engagement by Non-Western female pursuit of studies in a male-dominated technological learning environment (Joseph, 2013).

Researchers believe that such single-gendered (female only) learning environment can assist Non-Western females to overcome anxiety and low-confidence when utilizing the online domain. However, there are not many learning environments that cater to Non-Western students, let alone Non-Western learning environment that cater to single-gendered students. This fosters for more dependency for Non-Western females to refrain from participating, disengage, or stay within the online domain for a limited amount of time. These barriers that trap the Non-Western female diminish her ability to assert herself in her own terms and gain the courage and confidence to speak for herself within the domain.

A CULTURE OF VOICELESSNESS: CONFIDENCE CHANGE AND IMPACT ON THE NWFC

Due to the foreign individualistic approach, language structure, intimidating technology structure of the online domain, the clash in cultural differences, and the Western perception of the Non-Western females as the "other" (Alcoff, 1991; Jaggar, 1998), the NWFC may find herself in a constant battle to express herself online as she already does in the physical world. These restrictions and differences in cultural upbringing will also create a chain reaction of constant negative experiences for the NWFC in the online world (Durndell & Thomson, 1997; Brody & Hall, 2000; Fels, 2004) and foster low confidence online. NWFC then withdraws further from the online domain and begins to fear situations of expression online. All women are not the same, some are diligent or timid and others determined (Winslow, 2010).

Although the nature of shyness and timidity may also be influential in silencing the NWFC and keeping her from expressing her concerns to corporate personnel through their CMC tools. In contrast, Non-Western females have been classified as strong (Oyewumi, 2002) and authoritative because of cultural upbringing and market strategies to sale and trade goods within market places consumer situations, and cultural life styles. For example, in Niara Sudarkasa's (1996) book she described African females, as not the "docile," "submissive," "downtrodden," powerless creatures they were perceived to be. African females were rulers and leaders in all parts of Africa, with leaders like Nefertiti and Cleopatra (Sudarkasa, 1996). There are many discussions on the black female's other roles in Africa as land and farm owners. Her strength was prominent and celebrated (Boserup, 2007). The black female's strength was not only apparent in the public sphere before her arrival to the Americas, as slaves, and after her arrival, through the harsh labor roles the black female was seen within the family and community as strong mentally. This strength may show in her interactions online even with the unfamiliar territory of the online domain. In contradiction to this strength that the Non-Western female may possess, the foreignness of the online domain showcases that when approached in a new environment, conflict avoidance becomes more apparent as the best approach (Harper, 2004; Maravelas, 2005; Wilmot & Hocker, 2007). The new environment can limit her expression online causing her to be seen by Western observers as shy and timid.

In the domains of Western language foundations, male perceived technical structure, and Western cultural components, the Non-Western female finds herself in a difficult circumstance voicing her concerns and opinions. Hence, the Non-Western female keeps away from engaging in online situations and finds them unfavorable. Although this may be the case by some researchers, other researchers believe that the power of word-of-mouth allows any individual to express grievances and concerns to other, especially online, where the consumer has the most control. Such cases as musician Dave Carroll United Breaks Guitars, demonstrated the power of customers on social media to communicate their complaints and be heard by millions of YouTube viewers and national news channels (Carroll, 2012). Such an act is considered as progress because one continues to reach out to be heard, even if it is not directed to the corporation. Alternatively, this manner of "being heard" is not the same as being heard by the corporations the NWFC is having the conflict with. She must be creative and understand the process of marketing (Carroll, 2012; Smith, Fischer, & Yongjian, 2012) to promote her social media message. In addition, many researchers asserted that the NWFC is far from the typical online user (Harding, 1997, Joiner et al., 2005) and therefore is unable to generate the same type of word-of-mouth as other users who are familiar and have "lived" (Harding, 1997, 1998; Li & Kirkup, 2007) in the web domain for an extensive period of time (Harding, 1997, 1998; Joiner et al., 2005).

The cultural dynamics of the Non-Western female's life consists of structures that have been implemented and constructed to restrict her speech,

expression, opinion, and even thoughts. She is already, by her physical surroundings, diminishing her ability to speak and be heard in her own terms. In
some NWFC cultures, their speech is expressed to their husbands and in other
cultures their speech is expressed to their local communities (Li & Kirkup,
2007). In Olu Pearce essay (1999) she focused on the social construction
of infertility and childlessness in women among the Yoruba tribe of South-
western Nigeria based on two empirical studies conducted in Ijero-Ekiti and
Ibadan. Pearce (1999) illustrates one of the many battles that females in Nigeria face. She stated, "Childless women have historically been held in great
contempt in Yorubaland. Today, as in the past, children ensure the status and
future of the patrilineage, a wife's infertility remains the concern of the whole
group, becoming both a personal and a public issue" (Pearce, 1999, p. 1).

Furthermore, Nigerian females are among other Non-Western females who
have these cultural circumstances attached to childbirth. They feel uncared
for and disrespected by their wider kin. They also complain that children they
fostered do not, as a rule, come forward to help them in their old age (Larsen,
Obono, & Whitehouse, 2009). On the other hand, some researchers believe that
Western influence on these cultures will enlighten those who practice Non-
Western cultures (West, 1990; Huntington, 1993; Kapoor, 2002) to be more
accepting of the community members and the Internet will allow this progress
of changing the minds of those who gain access to the Western domain.

On the contrary, the online domain seems to offer another male structured
dynamic with its own set of rules that place females once again at a disadvan-
tageous position. Some scholars believe that females are seen in the Western
world as "bitchy" or "manly." In the Non-Western world, females are also
perceived negatively if they are assertive and expressive in areas that are not
related to child rearing or home management. Females always find themselves losing. Ezumah (2008) explained this concept as it pertains to Yoruba
and Cameroun traditions, describing how women are faced with many challenges and contradictions in their efforts to attain self-actualization. Women
are said to have "O ti ra ni ye" which means in the Yoruba expressions that
the husband has been bewitched by the wife or "ti so didnrin" which also implies that the woman has so bewitched the man that he has lost his intellect.
Nigeria is not the only country where individuals express this idea of regarding women's endeavor to gain status, power and wealth in negative terms.
Kaberry (1952, 46) referred to the reluctance of men in Bamenda, Cameroun
to accept women in male dominated trade. The men expressed fears that such
a trend will disturb the joint dependence that existed between wife and husband, in addition to undermining the stability of marriage.

On the other hand, researchers recognize that cultural norms contribute in
defining the manner in which genders are treated, such as sexual violence

(Kalof, 2000; Singleton, 2004). In the hopes of allowing expression for the Non-Western female, the online domain presents a cultural clash (Huntington, 1993) which may provide the NWFC, who live in cultures where female expression is suppressed the chance to start expressing themselves. On the contrary, Abraham (2000) described how the primary culture overshadows any new interfering cultures. For example, the South Asian cultural norms have been defined as a collection of values, behaviors, and meanings held by a group as they create their interpretations of the world. Researchers acknowledge that cultural norms play a role in defining sexual violence. African family culture (Oyewumi, 2002) as well as South Asian notions of family are often distinctly different than those in the U.S., where "the family and group-oriented structure views the individual as a representative of the family . . . and there is considerable pressure to maintain harmony and minimize any actions that would potentially jeopardize the family and community" (Abraham, 2000, p. 19).

On the contrary, outside of culture and traditions, other studies have illustrated the female's interest to engage in self-expression because she feels that she will not be heard. Brody and Hall (2000) asserted that females are more inclined to have emotional attachment to events and experience influencing them to want to avoid such negative past experiences, which can prevent them from wanting to re-explore past negative situations and experiences. This emotional attachment can create a rippling effect influencing the female to distance herself from situations that will cause negative emotions (Freud, 1895). She then limits her exposure to the environment, individual(s), and circumstances that have caused past negative emotions and feelings. Brody and Hall (2000) also found in their research that females have reported themselves as experiencing more intense emotions than males reported, and females are more willing to self-disclose about emotions.

In conclusion, not being heard or understood diminishes the expression of the NWFC as much as it would be for anyone who had always experienced mistreatments and lacked in expression, concerns, complaints, needs and wants. In the online environment, a negative Western corporation experience may diminish the NWFC's voice in expressing her concern to corporate personnel online. If these experiences occur frequently, her confidence is lowered and the ability to express is further diminished. In addition, the cultural ways of expression is beyond the online structure for the NWFC as she focuses on expressing her concern to her local community where she feels welcomed and her expression is without Western constructs and follows her already established cultural set norms.

Chapter Three

Methodology

INTRODUCTION

In a world where the female outside of the Western sphere for centuries has been a business owner by birth (or farmer, trader, and laborer), where the female consumer has leverage in voicing her opinion on consumer goods and influential in market sales, she faces an environment that is foreign to her where her voice and expression can be diminished or worst, unheard and seen by Westerns as muted. With many cultures outside the West, the Non-Western female consumer (NWFC) is bombarded by the Western dominated consumer culture when connecting to online marketplaces. This study answers four research questions: RQ1. Does lack of self-confidence diminish the Non-Western female consumer's voice in expressing her concerns to Western corporations through their computer-mediated communication tools? RQ2. How do cultural differences diminish the Non-Western female consumer's voice in expressing her concerns to Western corporations through their computer-mediated communication tools? RQ3. How do language barriers diminish the Non-Western female consumer's voice in expressing her concerns to Western corporations through their computer-mediated communication tools? RQ4. Have social media platforms changed the Non-Western female consumer's complaint behavior and her actions in expressing her concerns through other venues?

The methodology approach of this study was designed to answer four research questions in order to evaluate the Non-Western female consumer's confidence level, cultural influence, and Western language domination impact on her ability to express her concerns to Western corporation personnel through Western corporation's computer-mediated communication (CMC) tools and online social media platforms. Focus on analyzing and interpreting the Non-Western female consumer's lack of ability to express her concerns through corporate CMC tools to corporation personnel is imperative to the study. This proposition was based on the concept of understanding the Non-Western female consumer's online conflict and complaint existence through her view of the online domain, and aims to give insight to her reasoning and approach to disengage and distance herself from a dissatisfied Western corporations, corporate CMC support tools and personnel. This study explored specific confidence elements and causes of lack of confidence, which include unfamiliarity with online domain structure and culture (Western based). This study also examined the Non-Western female consumer's online complaint strategies with Western corporations versus her in-person complaint to local native businesses, examined and compared cultural norms, dominate language structure and self-confidence changes.

This chapter defined the details and specifics of the study, and set forth the processes and methods used, including its method of sampling, research design, and its instrumentation, data collection and analysis, reliability, and ethical considerations. In the anticipation to explore and examine cross-cultural and gender consumer problems, solve the Non-Western female consumer (NWFC) online consumer-to-business conflict communication pattern, educate Western corporation's on their online business-to-consumer communication problems, build the NWFC's confidence, defuse the NWFC and Western corporations business-to-consumer conflict anxiety, this study utilized the interview method as the most appropriate and precise observation for the targeted research group. Furthermore, in the hopes to give presence, reveal, evaluate and understand the NWFC's online world and her perspective, this study utilized the interview approach as a methodology and in-depth interview protocol as the instrument to elicit data from participants.

RESEARCH METHOD

Each method has its advantages and disadvantages, however, selecting the type of research methodology to utilize is one of the most critical decisions a researcher can make. The qualitative and quantitative research methods permit researchers to explore and locate the needed information to solidify their research (Frey, Boton, Kreps, 2000; Hellsten, Preston, Prytula, & Jeancart, 2014; Ivankova & Clark, 2018). However, the two research approaches give way for difference types of research studies. In particular, when conducting communication research, both qualitative and quantitative method can be utilized. However, the determining factor is based on the approach that suits the study, and the method that will produce reliable results. These research methods are identified by the researcher. In the selection, the most important part is deciding on the most appropriate and effective approach to investigate the study (Trafimow, 2014).

In the exploratory study of the NWFC the advantages and structure of the qualitative method allows the NWFC to be evaluated through her Non-Westernized cultural norms, which is essential in this study. Not only did the qualitative method allow room for a more complete analysis of the NWFC's perspective (Ardener, 1975) as it pertains to online complaint confidence, social media usage for corporate complaints (Katz, 1959), it also provided an effective manner to begin to understand the lens through which the NWFC views the online domain. By utilizing qualitative research, the NWFC was provided an avenue to express her view point without Western restricted quantitative tools such as questionnaire, but allows an unstructured Western approach which promotes her expression through her cultural norms and in her own expression and terms. Through this structure the NWFC is able to illustrate her view of the global domain, her position within it, and define the boundaries and walls (i.e. cultural clashes or unfamiliarity, etc.) she believes chain and bind her from addressing her concerns, complaints, and opinions online. As a result of the opportunity the qualitative method provides to give presence to the NWFC, it was implemented to give a snapshot of:

1. concerns of NWFC interview participants within selected countries (China, Nigeria, and India);
2. issues that distance her involvement in expressing her concerns and directly communicating to the Western corporations online;
3. how corporate CMC tools and personnel involvement differentiates her behavior to voice her complaints compared to local native business personnel;
4. and understand the perspective of the NWFC by allowing her to speak.

RATIONALE FOR RESEARCH DESIGN STRATEGY

Introducing the online world of the NWFC was done with a research method that allowed the NWFC to express the difficulties she encounters online. Gaining familiarity with the NWFC, her struggles, obstacles and concerns, the design of this study, gave her a full advantage of self-expression. This study allowed the NWFC to speak without restriction and provided detailed observation and characteristics of the NWFC. The research methodology that allowed for adequate and close examination of the targeted NWFC group is qualitative research. Qualitative research has been defined (Bogdan & Biklen, 2007; Hatch, 2002) through several characteristics including:

1. Naturalistic-Qualitative researchers go to a particular setting for the direct source of data because of their concern for accurate context;
2. Participant Perspectives-Qualitative research, the voices of the participants predominate;
3. Descriptive Data-Qualitative research usually takes the form of pictures or words rather than numbers;
4. Meaning-Qualitative researchers are interested in how people make sense of their lives;
5. Researcher as Data Gathering Instrument-Qualitative researcher as interprets through field notes, interview translations and observations are collected by the investigator;
6. Wholeness and Complexity-Allows researcher to systematically look at social contexts in a holistic approach.

Qualitative purists, who are also known as interpretivists and constructivists, argue for the superiority of constructivism, relativism, idealism, humanism, and hermeneutics. "These purists contend that multiple-constructed realities abound, time-and context-free generalizations are neither desirable nor possible, research is value-bound, and it is impossible to differentiate fully causes and effects" (Johnson & Onwuegbuzie, p. 14, 2006). Lindorf and Taylor (2011) asserted that, "Qualitative research theory is best developed inductively" (p. 8–9). It utilizes theory in much more varied ways. The method in which theory is used in qualitative research affects its placement. A theory that comes at the beginning provides a lens that shapes the object of study and the questions asked (such as in ethnographic research). Sometimes, the researcher may generate a theory as the final outcome of the study and place it at the end of a project (such as in grounded theory). Furthermore, qualitative research can enhance understanding and expand theoretical knowledge from a disciplinary perspective. By utilizing the qualitative method researchers can begin to understand the personal pains, struggles and perspective of individuals and groups/cultures. Qualitative researchers can obtain thicker descriptions (Onwuegbuzie & Byers, 2014).

Qualitative research data is based on the participants' own sets of meaning, its practicality for studying a limited number of participants and cases in both detail and in-depth, its usefulness for illustrating, evaluation, analyzing, and describing complex phenomena in depth, and it provides individual detailed case information (Lindorf and Taylor, 2011). In addition, qualitative research provides understanding and description of people's lens, viewpoints, unique perspectives, personal experiences, and involvement with a phenomenon (Onwuegbuzie & Byers, 2014).

Participants within the qualitative approach lend themselves to exploring why and how a phenomenon occurs. Some of the weaknesses of qualitative research include issues such as how the results it produced may not be generalizable to the overall population, and its findings may not be unique or match other individuals (Lindorf and Taylor, 2011). In qualitative research, hypotheses and theories are much more problematic to examine and results can easily be influenced by researcher's personal biases and idiosyncrasies. Furthermore, data collection, in many cases, is more time consuming, and it takes extensively more time to conduct data analysis (Johnson & Onwuegbuzie, 2006).

Notwithstanding the pros and cons, disadvantages and advantages of qualitative research, it is clear that the qualitative research methodology is tremendously beneficial in studying the NWFC. Unlike some studies where advantages of both methods together would heighten understanding and create a more complete evaluation (Langmia & Glass, 2014) in the case of the NWFC not only is qualitative research methodology the most suitable but it also gives the NWFC the ability to speak without restricting cultural norms of communication during the online interview process (i.e. non-verbal cues, face-to-face communication, personable approach). The qualitative research approach also allows the researcher to interpret and gain a more sufficient (Lindorf & Taylor, 2011) snapshot of the NWFC online consumer group. The qualitative approach also allows for better understanding of the NWFC, rather than constraining and restricting the online voice of the NWFC through quantitative methodology tools (Johnson & Onwuegbuzie, 2006).

In this study the only research methodology that has the features and elements that provided flexibility and embodied distinguishing characteristics of individuality as described in understanding the NWFC is the survey methodology design. The survey research method design is both a qualitative (interviews/open-questions) and a quantitative (questionnaires/close-questions) research methodology (Ivankova, 2014), and the best method available in research that observes, collects information, and perspectives of a few individuals, as well as, collects original data for describing a population too large to observe directly (Babbie, 2005; Ivankova, 2014). The survey approach which allows for in-depth interviewing was the most exhaustive method to acquire the desired knowledge sought in this study of the NWFC.

SURVEY METHODOLOGY DESIGN

Understanding the NWFC's online environment requires this study to tap into her online world by providing a platform for her to speak of her life online. It was imperative that the qualitative survey interview research approach be implemented to accommodate the NWFC. Utilizing interview method gave the NWFC the freedom to speak in an uncontrolled environment where she can provide information verbally, speak without reservation about her approach to online consumer complaint conflict, her culture complaint style, language barriers, and her self-confidence level in complaining to Western corporations. Only the NWFC can give us insight to understand if she feels like a stranger, a guest, a friend or family member in the online domain, and enlighten us about her world and specific experiences.

The qualitative research interview approach is most appropriate where individual perceptions of processes are explored within a social unit (such as a work group, department, or whole organization), and studied prospectively. The present study interviewed NWFCs. Each NWFC revealed her point-of-view, perspective, personal opinions, cultural stance, and provided information orally and visually. As a type of design in qualitative research, a case study methodology (Tipaldo, 2014), the interview approach is utilized mainly in the social sciences (popularity in medicine, law, and political science studies) and is also popular in psychology (Freud, 1895).

This current study evaluated, examined, and interpreted the perspective of NWFCs who are considered "mute" by Western observers. In order to completely gain comprehensive understanding of the NWFC's online view and evaluate the NWFC group in addressing the Western classified "mute" phenomenon, the qualitative approach was utilized. In this present study, in-depth interview questions were utilized (Dillman, Smyth, & Christioan, 2009). The interview approach assisted in identifying how situational factors and context affect the NWFC participant's online experience and behavior (McEvoy, Ballini, Maltoni, O'Donnell, Mair, & MacFarlane, 2014). The interview approach facilitated in gathering in-depth detail of situations and instances that increased or established a diminished voice online for the NWFC. It gave a deeper level of descriptive detail that permitted the qualitative results to be analyzed to express the NWFC's perspective (Brueton, Stevenson, Vale, Stenning, Tierney, Harding, & Rait, 2014).

Since many Non-Western females may not be online Western corporation consumers, the NWFCs were selected through purposive sampling to speak from their perspectives as online shoppers. Each NWFC spoke of her own online domain experience and perspective through this study. The study used the in-depth interview approach to allow the NWFC to express her opinion and thoughts, and give clarity and understanding of how her self-confidence, culture and language difference influences her actions when speaking with Western personnel through corporations' online CMC tools. These interviews were one-on-one in-depth interviews (Denzin & Lincoln, 2011). The following research questions were posed: RQ1. Does lack of self-confidence diminish the Non-Western female consumer's voice in expressing her concerns to Western corporations through their computer-mediated communication tools? RQ2. How do cultural differences diminish the Non-Western female consumer's voice in expressing her concerns to Western corporations through their computer-mediated communication tools? RQ3. How do language barriers diminish the Non-Western female consumer's voice in expressing her concerns to Western corporations through their computer-mediated communication tools? RQ4. Have social media platforms changed the Non-Western female consumer's complaint behavior and her actions in expressing her concerns through other venues?

SAMPLE AND SAMPLING METHOD

While quantitative research utilizes probability sampling, non-probability sampling (known also as non-random sampling) is used in qualitative research. The major drawback of non-probability sampling is that the researcher does not know each participant's probability of being selected for the study. Qualitative research cannot state that the participants can represent the entire population, which reduces the possibility of generalizing the findings (Handcock & Gile, 2010).

Non-probability sampling has several types of sampling approaches including convenience sampling (known also as accidental, availability, haphazard sampling). It is the least rigorous technique and involves the selection of the most accessible subjects. Quota sampling was created to assist in overcoming the error of availability sampling. In quota sampling an effort is made to ensure distribution of demographic variables. Subjects are recruited as they arrive and assigned to demographic groups centered on particular variables (e.g. age and sex). Once the quota for a given demographic group is filled, the recruiting process for that particular group ends (Flick, 2014). Purposive sampling (also known as judgment sampling) allows the researcher to select the most productive sample to answer the research questions. This is the most common sampling technique (Gjoka, Kurt, Butts, & Markopoulou, 2010). Purposeful sampling selects subjects based on purpose of the study, characteristics, and gathers data from cases for in-depth examination of the study. The researcher samples with a purpose of the research objective in mind.

Purposive sampling is popular in qualitative research. There are many different types and techniques of purposeful sampling, including homogeneous and opportunistic sampling, and many other types and combination or mixed purposeful (mixture of several types of purposive sampling) sampling which provides flexibility, triangulation, multiple interests, and needs of different research studies. A popular subset of purposive sample is snowball sampling.

Snowball sampling technique allows researchers to identify potential subjects in a study if subjects are hard to locate. The researcher seeks assistance from already interviewed participants to give referrals of others who are a good example of the study or could enrich the study (Flick, 2014). The researcher may identify one member of the population of interest or speak with individuals interested in the study and then asks them to help identify subjects that fit the study criteria. The researcher identifies cases of study interest from people who know others who would be excellent interview subjects.

Since this study focused on the NWFC, the purposive sample approach was utilized in order to recruit NWFCs. The difficulty to locate the special minority group members (who were Non-Western females that engaged in Western online consumption) initiated the use of the snowball sampling. Targeting the NWFC required seeking the patterns, characteristics, actions and behavior of consumer experiences that fit the NWFC. It also required seeking those who know the NWFC to identify her. Although obstacles, conditions and characteristics may distance the NWFC from addressing Western personnel through established CMC tools and speaking about their experiences and complaints with Western corporations online, however, the NWFC may utilize word-of-mouth (communication with family and friends, and online avenues such as social media platforms) to express her concerns to others.

The number of NWFC interview participants was determined through data saturation. The concept of saturation was first defined in the context of grounded theory as "theoretical saturation" (Glaser & Strauss, 1967, p. 61). Since then the word has been used almost interchangeably with such terms as data saturation and conceptual saturation, the meaning of saturation has become blurred. "Saturation of knowledge" (Bertaux, 1981, p. 37) is a better term as saturation is simply defined as data satisfaction. Saturation of knowledge is when the research is surprised or learns a great deal from the interviews, reaches a point where no new information is obtained from further data, and recognizes patterns in the interviewees' experiences. More interviews ratify what the researcher has already detected.

Using purposive sampling and snowball sampling, saturation of knowledge was reached at 18 adult NWFCs. In all, 6 NWFCs from China, 6 NWFCs from Nigeria, and 6 NWFCs from India were interviewed on issues of Western corporation interaction, behavior during complaining about consumer dissatisfactions, online complaint approaches when dissatisfied with Western corporations, and local native business personnel communication versus Western online communications when discussion conflict and concerns. The international distance and cultural communication attributes of the NWFCs required that the interviews be conducted through virtual travel (carried on by means of computer networks-virtual conversations in a chatroom), utilizing CMC platforms and social media websites: email; mobile messaging; and online video and audio-taping equipment. Appendix B shows the interview questions for the NWFC.

INSTRUMENTATION

Virtual Travel: Mobile Message, Email and Online Video Interviewing

Through in-depth interviewing, the NWFC was allowed to voice her opinion about reasons why she did not communicate with Western corporations through their CMC tools. It also allowed her to discuss the actions she took instead of speaking with Western corporations. The study conducted 30 minute individual interviews with 18 NWFCs. These interviews were conducted via email and social media platforms: international mobile messaging application-WhatsApp, online video and audio-taping equipment (Skype, Facebook chat, and Google Hangouts). In the interview process, choosing the style of question to ask was important not only for the results, but also for the ethical foundation and reliability of the research. The purpose of the interview questions was to better understand the NWFC, which required the selection of questions that gave the NWFC full control of expression.

During the interviews, using semi-structured questions allowed for better selection of wording for each question to give the NWFC better understanding of the question. In addition, utilizing semi-structured questions also allows for new questions to be formulated during the interview. There are a few disadvantages of using the semi-structured questions approach. One major disadvantage to semi-structured questions is that with certain questions, semi-structured questions can be manipulated to embrace the researcher's view points and restrict free speech from participants. With semi-structured interviewing, certain answers are impossible to obtain due to how the questions are framed. For example, if the researcher asks a respondent 'how she felt' during a medical procedure, the researcher is invoking the category 'emotion.' Whatever the respondent chooses to say will have an emotional attachment (Willig, 2001; Willig, 2013).

The semi-structured interview approach has a framework of themes to be explored. While the structured interview approach has a formalized, limited set of questions, a semi-structured interview is flexible and allows the interviewer to ask new questions during the interview process reflecting to further investigate upon what the respondent says (Robson, 2011). This approach provides the interviewer the advantage to probe further and dig deeper to better understand the respondent. It adds and enriches the research

and promotes interaction between the interviewer and interviewee. It generated more detailed knowledge about the research scope and the researched
minority group of NWFCs.

In the NWFC study, semi-structured questions were utilized. All semi-
structured questions that were posed to the NWFC are on the questions
list (See Appendix B). The interview protocol served as a guide for
interviewing the NWFC participants and not every interview question
was appropriate for each of the NWFCs. Instead of developing different
interview questions for each participant, a single interview question guide
was utilized with several questions pertaining to the scope of the present
NWFC study. Depending on the participant's answer and point-of-view,
experience, level of understanding in regards to the variables, characteristics, and answers, some of the questions were omitted or selected as appropriate questions to ask during the online video interviews. By utilizing
semi-structured questions, the NWFCs invited us into her world, a journey
(Lugones, 1993) to hear, learn, and understand her perspective on online
sphere, Western corporation personnel and CMC tools, social media platforms, and her conflict, complaint, struggles and challenges on the web
sphere. She explained her reasoning and behavior in complaint approaches,
and if and how much she believes her lack of self-confidence impacts her
online communication interactions.

GENERAL SELF-EFFICACY

In order to observe the confidence of the NWFC and her ability to express
her concerns to Western corporations, the General Self-Efficacy (GSE)
question style was applied with the in-depth interview questions to evaluate
the extent to which each NWFC answers a particular question. The General
Self-Efficacy scale was created to evaluate an overall sense of Perceived
Self-Efficacy with the aim to predict coping with daily hassles as well as adaptation after experiencing different types of stressful life events (Schwarzer
& Jerusalem in, 1995).

Self-efficacy has become a widely studied variable in the educational,
psychological, and organizational sciences (Scherbaum, Cohen-Charash, &
Kern, 2006) for the past 20 years. Self-efficacy is defined as a person's belief
in his or her ability to muster the cognitive, motivational, and behavioral
resources required to perform in a given situation. Self-efficacy is a situation-
specific competence belief. Its popularity rests on the research that confirmed
that self-efficacy is related to a number of educationally and organizationally
relevant variables (i.e. academic and job performance). GSE and self-esteem

are general self-evaluation concepts and hence should be substantially correlated. Self-esteem is a more affective concept whereas GSE is a more motivational concept (Chen, Gully, & Eden, 2001). Ralf Schwarzer elaborated on the Perceived Self-Efficacy and GSE scale. Perceived Self-Efficacy is the belief that a person has the ability to perform a difficult task, novel or cope with adversity. Perceived Self-Efficacy facilitates goal-setting, effort investment and persistence in the face of obstacles, barriers, and recovery from setbacks. It can be considered as a positive resistance source factor. Perceived Self-Efficacy is an operative construct, which means that it is related to subsequent behavior and is relevant for behavior change and clinical practice (Schwarzer, 2010).

The GSE scale is intended for the universal adult population. In regards to reliability, the scale samples 23 nations. In regards to validity, criterion-related validity is documented in numerous correlation studies where positive coefficients were found with favorable emotions, dispositional optimism, and work satisfaction. Negative coefficients were found with depression, anxiety, stress, and burnouts. The advantages of the GSE scale include how it has been used internationally with success for two decades. It is suitable for a broad range of applications and can be used to predict adaptation after life changes. It is also suitable as an indicator of quality of life at any point in time. The GSE scale's disadvantage is that it is a general measure, it does not tap specific behavior change (i.e. NWFC utilizing social media as a complaint platform for her dissatisfactions). Therefore, in most applications it is necessary to add a few items to cover the particular content of the survey or intervention (Schwarzer, 2010) (such as social media as a self-efficacy propeller).

The psychometric properties associated with the GSE have been criticized. Such criticism has hindered efforts to further establish the construct of GSE. Contrary to the criticisms, Scherbaum, Cohen-Charash, and Kern study measures of GSE demonstrated acceptable psychometric properties. Their results indicated that the New General Self-Efficacy scale has a slight advantage over the other measures used to determine individuals' belief in their performance abilities (Schwarzer & Jerusalem, 1995). Although health psychology (the study of psychological and behavioral processes in health, mental health, etc.) is the foundation of GSE scale, the scale has been used for other studies (Scherbaum, Cohen-Charash, & Kern, 2006), which focused on individuals' belief in their ability to perform well in a variety of situations which is the foundation of GSE. In this study, the General Self-Efficacy question style assisted in structuring the interview questions in order to evaluate the extent to which each NWFC answers a particular question that was related to self-confidence and ability.

QUALITATIVE MEASURES FOR ANALYSIS

The NWFC interview questions created for this present study was used to evaluate how the Western culture influence of the online domain structure affects the NWFC in three aspects: complaint self-confidence level behavior/ confidence level change, influence of cultural norms, and language barriers impact on the NWFC while using corporate complaint CMC tools verses social media platforms. As described and illustrated by Robert Yin (2003; 2014), whose Case Study Tactics has been discussed and duplicated a plethora amount of times by other researchers (Versendaal, van den Akker, Xing, & de Bevere, 2013; Schaarschmidt & Kilian, 2014; Cronin, 2014), a detail recommended range of tactics utilized to judge the quality of case study research is mandatory when seeking to understand validity and reliability.

In-depth interview questions and narratives from the 18 NWFCs were the primary source of evidence for this current study. In addition, the snowball approach was utilized to recruit NWFC interview participants. A chain of evidence was maintained from the notes taken during the NWFC interviews. The notes included online video recording, audio tapes, hand written notes (e.g. written during interviews) and typed notes (e.g. notes written after the interview and prepared as consequence of document analysis procedures). The study documents included information sheets, participants' contact data sheet, interview schedules (based on NWFC participant's local time), interview questions, and emails confirming times and dates of interviews and records of follow-up activities (e.g. thank you notes).

A written guide was used to carry out data collection procedures protocol. In addition, the protocol included the following: providing the 18 NWFCs with a summary of the research project (e.g. objectives and background information) and developing field procedures, (e.g. snowball sampling), obtaining resources (email, mobile messaging tools like WhatsApp, online video and audio-taping equipment like Skype, Facebook chat, and Google Hangouts), and scheduling a timeline and date for data collection. Also, questions (which are the research question answered by the study) and a guide for the study were included.

After the 18 interviews were completed, the interviews were translated. The study database included the collection of notes, video and voice (online video and tape recording) observation, documents, materials, and interview notes (before and after interview, which allowed for an organized study, with respect to maintain a chain of evidence for determining construct validity. Within the context of bias and limitations to qualitative research study were considered (Obradovich, 2009). In order to fulfill these considerations, essential steps and other precautions were addressed in the current study. Since the NWFCs were recruited through snowball sampling, the researcher had very little contact with any of the participants before the study. Disclosure of previous or present relationships between researcher and the participants in the study was limited. This study's sampling selection was purposeful with a small number of cases (18 adult NWFCs).

Although in qualitative research there are some concerns about bias about the interview approach which indicates a tendency for informants to articulate responses that are perceived to be agreeable to the researcher, and the elaboration of the participant's answers, however, the confidence the participant has to express themselves in the research can promote their ability to speak and be heard through research (passive aggressive) regardless of the bias attached through questions. The snowball technique allowed the participants to speak and answer honestly without attachment to researcher or research bias and also speak of their perspectives without a filter, a reprimand or intimidation. Furthermore, the design phase of the research was created with focuson the NWFCs' emotional well-being while being interviewed (Obradovich, 2009).

Also, the answers from the narratives provided by the 18 NWFC interview participants were reported as is and not changed but was kept as the NWFCs asserted. In order to make the meaning of statements easier to grasp verbal fillers like "um," or false starts to sentences were eliminated from transcription of responses. Furthermore, since this present study is partially objective, the researcher remained as objective as possible in the interpretation of the results. Moreover, the professional and the research approach manner that connected the interviewees and the researcher due to the snowball sampling approach assisted in preventing biases and potential threats to the validity of the findings. In addition, the interview transcriptions were reviewed by the researcher and a research assistant for accuracy of participants' recorded words. To further verify accuracy of interview questions, each participant verified their own answer responses to the interview questions they provided during their interview session and received a copy of their transcript. Each participant was invited to review her transcript and make any changes that she felt was necessary to make her responses clear. This review verified the accuracy of the transcripts.

NVIVO CODING AND THEMES

After the clarifications or changes were made and re-submitted by the NWFCs, the transcripts were loaded into Excel and QSR NVivo 10 for coding. When the coding was completed, the data was transformed into clusters of meanings and put into topic themes. Afterwards, the interview text, video and audio recordings were uploaded to Microsoft Word and coded in QSR NVivo 10 (Obradovich, 2009). The use of Microsoft Excel and QSR NVivo 10 software applications allowed for the data to be organized, sorted, categorized and coded for data analysis. The interview data collection material was analyzed, which allowed for topic (issues being discussed), analytical (relation to research questions), and case (assign demographic attributes) coding, generate themes and the connections between themes and the research questions.

This present study followed a set of steps for the structure of sequences of data collections (Obradovich, 2009) for interviews. The set of steps included:

1. Purposefully interviewed participants until saturation of knowledge was reached, gathered 18 NWFCs.
2. Mobile text messaged, emailed, online chatted, or video recorded the interviews (interview method was based on participants' preferences).
3. Transcribed and reviewed interviews with an unbiased research assistant's help.
4. Compared transcribed interviews and notes for consistency, accuracy, and understanding.
5. Allow interviewees to review their individual transcript.
6. Uploaded the open-ended questions and recorded interview transcripts and notes into Excel and QSR NVivo 10.
7. Organized and coded data material in QSR NVivo 10.
8. Categorized themes and trends identified in interviews and notes.

ETHICAL CONSIDERATIONS

In compliance with ethical practices of research, prior to each NWFC participant's interview, the following statement was provided to them: "Completion of the survey is voluntary. You may withdraw your participation at any time prior to returning it to the investigators. Refusal to participate will not have any negative consequences for you whatsoever. Completion of this questionnaire implies consent to participate in this project." During the interview sessions, the NWFC interview participants were guaranteed that their real names would not be used. Only their country, age, gender, ethnicity, and method of interview were noted. Appendix C shows the "Non-Western Female Consumer Interview Consent Form." On the online interview consent form, it was made clear to the participants that any personal information resulting from the research study was kept strictly confidential.

All Non-Western female subjects who participated in the online video interview were given detailed information and the reasons for the research and the importance of their participation. There was no deception to the subjects. There was no debriefing because it was not necessary. The online video interview was intended for Non-Western females who could speak English moderately good to adequately and those who can read, understand, hear, and express themselves in the English language moderately good to adequately. It was expected that the NWFCs were familiar with the English language (reading and speaking) enough to participate in the study, since the majority of CMC and social media websites are English based and English language is used frequently and in some cases a requirement in the selected countries of the study. Words within the interview questions were simplified during the interview process to promote the understanding of the questions being asked to the participants. Since the nature of the study was focused on the NWFC, it was expected that some of the participants may not be able to write in the English language or speak in English as adequately as a Western female Provisions were made so that each NWFC was not required to write English well or speak English well since the online video interviewing allowed her to speak her answers or type her answers.

Chapter Four

Analysis

INTRODUCTION

In the quest to find out if Non-Western female consumers, who were born, raised, and live in China, India, and Nigeria are affected by cultural norms, language barriers, or self-confidence when expressing their concerns to Western corporations' through their computer-mediated communication and utilizing social media to express concerns about Western corporations, in-depth interviews were carried out until "saturation of knowledge" (Bertaux, 1981, p. 37; Boyer et al., 2018) was reached. In all, 18 individual interviews were conducted. The duration of the interviews lasted approximately 30 minutes each. The 18 interviewees were Non-Western female consumer (NWFC) participants who classified themselves as online Western consumers. The NWFCs were selected through snowball sampling.

Each NWFC's interview was scheduled in the local standard time where the interviewee resided and at a time when it was most convenient for the interviewee. Questions were tailored to focus on the NWFC's expressed concerns on communicating with Western corporations' through their online tools. The broad interview questions allowed participants to freely express themselves. The interview questions also supported participants in further elaborating on their major concerns in communicating with Western corporations. The use of in-depth interviewing enabled the flow of participants' descriptions and rich data collection. Each online video audio file was transcribed and emailed to interviewees in order to check accuracy. Data management was supported by QSR NVivo 10. Open coding was used until the related and core categories had emerged, whereupon selective coding was conducted. Each NWFC received a number code (e.g. NWFC-Nigeria1) that identified her.

After these descriptions were gathered, the reflected interactions between the Non-Western females and their actions in communicating through Western corporations' online tools in correspondent with consumership complaints were explored. The main factors that limited the NWFC's online interaction with Western corporations were noted in one or more of the interviewed Non-Western female consumers. These factors assisted in explaining the barriers that restrict the NWFC from expressing her concerns to Western corporation's online tools as well as expressing her concern on social media platforms when she is dissatisfied with Western products or services.

NWFC INTERVIEW PARTICIPANTS DEMOGRAPHIC DESCRIPTIONS AND IDENTIFICATION

The NWFC interview participants indicated that they were all online shoppers or have participated in online shopping at some point within the last two years. Their ability to shop online and use social media sites contributed to their ability to be participants of the study. With each NWFC defining her specific behavior traits and her reasons for utilizing or not utilizing Western corporation's online tools to express her concerns, it was clear that the components that defined her ability also defined her behaviors in expressing her concerns to Western companies. All the NWFCs were frequent local shoppers in their perspective country. Furthermore, all of the participants spoke English fluently, near-fluently, moderately, or minimally well to a degree that they could express their concerns and answer interview questions without use of an interpreter. Below is a list of the NWFC interview participants' country, age range, occupation, Western online shopping frequency, and their preferred contact platform for the interview (See Figure 4.1). In this study a NWFC who "shop online rarely" has shopped online 4 to 6 times within the last 2 years and a NWFC who "shop online often" has shopped more than 6 times within the last 2 years (See Figure 4.2).

NWFC-China1: Age 34, housewife, shops online often, Skype
NWFC-China2: Age 30, education specialist, shops online rarely, Skype
NWFC-China3: Age 26, marketing consultant, shops online often, Skype
NWFC-China4: Age 38, graduate student, shops online often, Skype
NWFC-China5: Age 34, graduate student, shops online often, Skype (text on Skype)
NWFC-China6: Age 40, firm statistics researcher, shops online rarely, Email
NWFC-Nigeria1: Age 40, housewife, shops online rarely, Skype

NWFC-Nigeria2: Age 43, bank teller, shops online rarely, Skype
NWFC-Nigeria3: Age 50, professor, shops online rarely, Phone
NWFC-Nigeria4: Age 42, business owner, shops online rarely, WhatsApp
NWFC-Nigeria5: Age 28, graduate student, shops online rarely, WhatsApp
NWFC-Nigeria6: Age 45, police officer, shops online rarely, WhatsApp
NWFC-India1: Age 54, professor, shops online rarely, Phone
NWFC-India2: Age 41, professor, shops online rarely, Phone
NWFC-India3: Age 30, dental assistant, shops online often, Skype
NWFC-India4: Age 33, technology firm manager, shops online often, Skype
NWFC-India5: Age 45, human resource manager, shops online rarely, Skype
NWFC-India6: Age 20, graduate student, shops online often, WhatsApp

In this study, when quoted, each interviewee was identified by her country and their given number. The given number represents the sequence in which she was interviewed. An example of interviewee identification is as follows: the participant who was interviewed first among the NWFCs from China was referred to as China1, the interviewee from Nigeria who was interviewed second among the NWFCs from Nigeria was referred to as Nigeria2, and the interviewee who was interviewed third among the NWFCs from India was referred to as India3. This applies to all the NWFC interviewees.

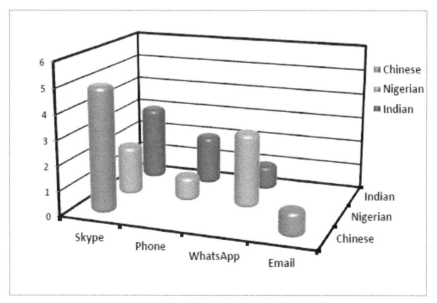

Figure 4.1. NWFC Interviewed Participants' Preferred Interview Contact Platform
Created by Chizoma C. Nosiri

Figure 4.2. NWFC Interviewed Participants' Online Shopping Frequency—Last Two Years
Created by Chizoma C. Nosiri

CONFLICTUAL REASONS THAT
DIMINISHED THE NWFC'S VOICE

In the process of understanding the NWFC's behavior and her relationship to communicating concerns to Western corporations and searching out answers to whether self-confidence, cultural structures or language barriers create conflictual reasons her voice was diminished in corporate complaint environment, a look at the themes derived from each NWFC's interview was significant. All of the 18 NWFC interview participants had access to a computer or a mobile device with online capability. They were all adequate in utilizing the Internet to shop and understood the dynamics of shopping online. All of the NWFC interview participants were between the ages of 23 and 54. The research revealed nine themes that emerged from the in-depth interviews which were central to the diminishing of the voices of the NWFCs when expressing their concerns to Western corporations. While all themes pertained to some NWFCs, a few were specific for some NWFC interview participants. The themes that diminished the NWFCs' voices in expressing their concerns to Western corporations through their online tools and also impacted their behavior in utilizing social media tools to express their concerns for Western corporation's services or products include (in level of greatness for the NWFC interview participants and subtheme categories):

Proactive Communication Confidence:
    Self-Efficacy and Ability

Cultural Clash:
  High and Context Culture
  Lack of Trust
  Historically and Globally Not Being Heard/Understood
  Conflict Avoidance: Unfamiliarity and Being Seen as the "Other"
  Individual Marketplace Strength/Collectivistic Approach
  Online vs. Local: An Ideal Cultural Blend
Language Barrier:
  The English Language Domination
Social Media:
  A Collectivistic Approach

Analysis
  Research Question 1: Does lack of self-confidence diminish the Non-Western female consumer's voice in expressing her concerns to Western corporations through their computer-mediated communication tools?
  Research Question 2: How do cultural differences diminish the Non-Western female consumer's voice in expressing her concerns to Western corporations through their computer-mediated communication tools?
  Research Question 3: How do language barriers diminish the Non-Western female consumer's voice in expressing her concerns to Western corporations through their computer-mediated communication tools?
  Research Question 4: Have social media platforms changed the Non-Western female consumer's complaint behavior and her actions in expressing her concerns through other venues?

PROACTIVE COMMUNICATION CONFIDENCE

Theme: Self-Efficacy and Ability

The theme "proactive communication confidence" was the key component and central element for almost all the NWFC interview participants' capability in communicating concerns to Western corporates. The theme, "proactive communication confidence" captured the meaning within the self-expression experience. If the experience was one that required contacting the Western corporation to express a concern, then the NWFCs were quick to engage in a communication with Western corporations. All but two NWFCs had a common reaction to Western corporation complaint communication ability protocol (See Figure 4.3). The influence to self-express a concern was the underlining factor behind the behavior and actions of the NWFC. There is an eagerness to connect with the Western corporations to express concerns as asserted by India3, "If they give their contact number then I would call them." Proactivity in self-expressing their concerns was a major concept that kept most of the NWFC interview participants involved in communicating to Western corporations about their concerns. Each of the NWFC interviewees explained how they felt about self-expression when they were unsatisfied with a Western product or service.

Q. Do you contact Western companies if you have a problem or a concern with their service or need to return a product?

> "Because it affected me, I do contact them." China4

> "If I'm not satisfied with the product I would probably contact them by email. I never feel like I am uncomfortable contacting Western companies." China5

> "If I found some problem with the product and the online connectivity is there then I will talk to them regarding the product. I think if it's their product they would want to know. They need to fix it. . . . I think the company will respond positively." India1

> "I would really like to give complements but if the product is really not good, I would like to give constructive feedback which will make them understand how they can improve with their product." India5

Many of the NWFC interview participants believed that confidence played a significant role in expressing their concerns to Western corporations. All of them expressed high confidence in communicating with Western corporations. They felt that they not only had a right to complain but owed it to

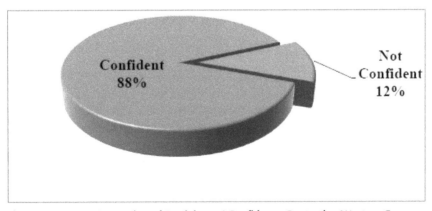

Figure 4.3.   NWFC Interviewed Participants' Confidence Contacting Western Corporations
Created by Chizoma C. Nosiri

the company, to tell them their wrong doings. Within the theme keywords derived from the NWFC interviews about confidence included high self-efficacy confidence number range of 5 and up (See Figure 4.4), returning/responding, not afraid, confident, and responsible and feedback.

Q. Do you think your confidence impacts your decision to express your concerns to unsatisfying Western companies? Are you confident with talking to Western companies if you had a problem?

"Yes I feel confident. No, I never feel afraid to contact the company. I can return the things I don't feel satisfied with. Even if I can't see them, I still return the products [with Amazon] if the products are really bad." China1

"If it's me I would call them directly to tell them about their product. If you buy something [say from Amazon] and it's not worth it, then you need to contact them. You don't want to spend money on something that is not worth it. I'm not afraid to contact them. I feel confident to speak about it." Nigeria1

"Yes, we have to provide feedback. Whatever we are expecting from that product and we don't get, we need to give some feedback. Whether it is a Western company or an Indian company, if they are responding, then it is fine." India3

Q. What is your confidence level when you express your concerns to Western companies'?

If you could rate your confidence 1–10, 10 being the highest, what would it be?

"Yes, I am confident, a 9. They may not solve all your problems but you do need to contact them." Nigeria3

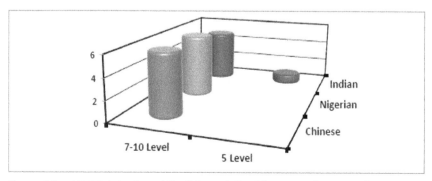

Figure 4.4. NWFC Interviewed Participants' Confidence Level—Contacting Western Corp.
Created by Chizoma C. Nosiri

"I would say my confidence is 7. I feel that I can handle the situation . . . when I have a problem. I feel that I am able to handle myself online. . . . I solve the problem by contacting them on their customer help tool online." Nigeria5

"I would say 7. I believe that I am confident and would talk to them." India2

"I would say 5 to 6. Definitely, there is a language issue. Language is a problem because I am not sure who will be answering there and how they would response and how they would talk to me." India3

"My confidence level is at 9. . . . I feel comfortable talking about the problem to have them solve it. . . . I usually return the things back. . . . I feel very comfortable calling them on the phone. I like to have them talk to me directly." India4

"Yes, I am confident, maybe 8. I can speak with anyone if I am facing any problem." India6

CULTURAL CLASH

Theme: High-Context Culture

The communication method of each NWFC participant varied; while some utilized Western email tools to communicate their concerns others preferred the phone method (See Figure 4.5). As expressed by India5 and many other interviewees the in-person format was desired. Already normalized cultural tendencies promoted many of the NWFC interviewees to feel that phone conversations, or even better, in-person communication gave them reassurance, comfort and a familiarity they were already use to. In some cases email was chosen to complete thought expression, lack of trust, and a paper trail evidence system which was expressed by Nigeria2, Nigeria5 and India5 respectively. Such obstacles like the online infrastructure and ability to readily connect online to phone cost reflect the difficulties for some of the NWFCs to communication their concerns to Western corporations. However, the desire to have a corporate representative who can directly be talked to in-person (many of the NWFC interview participants expressed this through the term "face-to-face") was paramount for most of the Nigerian and Indian women. As India5 stated, "It would be better if some representative would be here [in India] so the customer would talk to them personally."

On the other hand, established cultural expectations may be preconceived to be the similar response of Western companies who use Chinese personnel. As indicated by China4, "I think that the way people in America speak is different from China. Chinese are more personal. They get angry when you return an item in China," all of the Chinese NWFC interviewees had no desire to speak to Western corporation personnel by phone to express their concerns. Instead, their concern was on relaying their message accurately and completely without interruption, avoiding phone conversations conflict and language barrier issues. In contrast, China3 preferred to contact Western corporations' on their online website "chat" platform. The Western corporations the Chinese participants bought from were strictly Western corporations that had Chinese language capability. In order to buy from a Western corporation that was not restricted by Chinese online infrastructure or did not cater to Chinese language they utilized procurement services (a third-party individual, mainly Chinese who lived in the United States).

Email and Chat Preferred:

Q. Have you had any experience where you felt that you had a concern about a product or services or felt that you were mistreated, disrespect, or treated unfairly by a Western company (online or in person)? If so did you contact the Western company? How did you contact them?

> "I prefer chatting [online] with them because I can have record of what they say. I feel that chatting agents are more kind. They are more receptive and understanding, and more responsible in what they write in chat windows. . . . [America] customer services do not . . . . return email fast." China3

Q. Do you use email to contact Western companies when you have a concern?

> "I usually contact them online, by email. It is better for me to type. I usually type in Chinese." China1

> "Emailing takes a longer time [but it works]." China4

> "I will communicate with Western Company through e-mail because my listening and oral English is poor. . . . [Online] I will describe the situation in detail." China6

> "I prefer to contact the foreign company by email. It is easy for me. Their online emailing tools work for me. . . . They allow me to express my concerns completely and directly without any interruptions." Nigeria5

> "Email would be more convenient because you can write your concerns in detail through email. [However] if you could communicate with the product company directly, that is better. . . . [but] I prefer to have the local company communication style where you can communicate locally to the people. It is direct and you can see the face of the people, how that person's reaction would be and what clarification he or she would give back to you regarding your concern." India5

Phone Preferred:

Q. If you had any experience where you felt that you had a concern about a product or services, or felt that you were mistreated, disrespect, or treated unfairly by a Western company (online) how would you contact them?

"Typing is fine. It is just difficult to get a response. . . . The Internet is poor and very expensive. I use it at school. When I am at home, I can't use it because it is bad, so I prefer calling them. " Nigeria1

"I'll call and send an email as well. I think I want to send an email so I'll have evidence. The foreign companies also tell you this call is recorded for quality assurance. So, for that purpose I feel comfortable because I feel like somebody is listening and something can be done. But for most Nigerian companies no point in trying." Nigeria2

"I would call them over the phone because I will not be able to talk to them properly online. . . . It is better to hear them and talk to them directly. . . . I find it difficult to [email online] because of the barriers. Not being able to see them or know about the product and talking to them directly." India1

"I will surely contact [them] on their customer care number." India6

Q. Do you use email to contact Western companies when you have a concern?

"[I] would contact them by phone. [I] get to hear them talk to me." Nigeria6

"I don't find it easy to talk to foreign companies online. I find it easier to talk to them on the phone. . . . Local companies are better for me to talk with. I like the face-to-face approach and can talk to the local company about my problems and feel that they will be resolved." India2

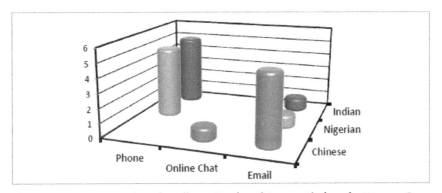

Figure 4.5.   NWFC Interviewed Partiipants' Preferred Contact Platform for Western Corp.
Created by Chizoma C. Nosiri

"Here [in India] actually phone is easier and faster in communicating so I would call them if I have their number. . . . You know, with phone it is answered in person. Someone will pick up the call and answer and they will probably see to the problem. . . . It is important because I don't want some machines answering me [but] not phone over face-to-face. Someone answering my problem personally is always better." India3

Theme: Lack of Trust

Trust and reliability were significant factors to the actions or lack of actions taken by the NWFC interview participants to contact Western corporations when expressing concerns about a product or service. All the countries had NWFC individuals that had past experiences that contributed to lack of trust or assumed that Western corporations were somehow untrustworthy (See Figure 4.6). Some of the NWFCs in Nigeria and India worried that their complaints would be irrelevant since viewing items physically was impossible so whatever they received they must accept. In addition, many Nigerian and Indian NWFC interviewees worried about honesty and reliability of online companies. The lack of country security structure that promoted thieves in Nigeria also caused concern to continue buying online for the interviewed Nigerian NWFCs. In China the scarceness of Western online corporations also prevented the interviewed Chinese NWFCs from seeking Western products and fostered a lack of trust for Western online corporations. The barriers of the Chinese online shopping structure, shopping through English websites and shopping through third party individuals leave many Chinese NWFCs unable to complain to Western corporations. This complicated dynamic was well described by Chian5 who relies on word-of-mouth from friends to find Western online companies and procurement service providers who are reliable to shop through, "I know little about [other Western online companies like Amazon] but I would buy from them if my friends told me it was good. The only way to shop foreign is through procurement service but you can't talk to them directly."

Q. Why don't you shop online often?

"My English is not good and people around me have no experience with Western companies so I don't want to get involved so I rather not complain." China4

"It's really security consciousness. I have heard of a lot of people around here, in Lagos, who have been robbed and I don't want to risk that, I have two young children. It's also difficult to ship things here [for returns] because it is more expensive and again security is a huge factor." Nigeria2

"I think that through online you might not get the service that you need. It may even fall into the hands of a wrong person. They might even advertise products and then when you give the money they might take the money and you might not receive the product. I use to get things from online ads but because I don't shop online that much anymore I just ignore the advertising. I don't trust Western company advertisement." Nigeria3

"In this part of the country, with Nigerian women, both the rich women and even some of the poor women would like to shop online but we like to go to the market to see the product, talk and [negotiate] price. Buying online we see that they will cheat us. We do not see the product we only see the online site and we don't know if it is the actual product that we want so we rather go to the market. You can't complain about something you can't touch or actually feel, and pricing the item with the dollar and the seller." Nigeria6

"I needed to buy a camera and somebody suggested I do online shopping. I thought about it but know it would not be the best idea because of the hassle of not knowing if it will be what I want since I can't see it." India1

"It is easier to talk to the local companies because it is face-to-face so I can go back and tell them what the problem is. I feel more comfortable . . . I have more confidence and trust with the local people." India4

Q. Have you ever been treated unfairly or badly by a Western company?

"Yes, I've had some problems. I order clothing for my baby who wears 2T but sometimes they send me 3T or they would tell me after I have confirmed my order that they are out of stock. . . . There were some companies that I have had some bad experiences and I say I will not contact them again. I felt mistreated. . . . Getting follow-up with Western companies is difficult. They waste my time but with Chinese companies if they make the same mistakes they would be really sorry about it and try to compensate not with money but I can feel that they really mean it. Maybe I feel like some of the Western companies discriminate. They can tell that my English is different and I might be more apologizing and kind when I write the email complaint, so they feel like 'Oh, it's ok to not say sorry to her that much,' as they do to Americans." China1

". . . sometimes I feel like they [sound] like they are nice but they don't want to take care of my problems so they give me an excuse for this or for that . . . But three days [later] I get no answer. I hate that kind of thing." China3

"I can say that the local companies when you go there, when they see you in person they take you more seriously . . . . So the local companies try to give more attention, [when you call Western companies] they don't take you seriously. They do not see how much you need it or how seriously you want it." Nigeria1

"I am not afraid of conflict and I am willing to directly contact foreign companies online but prefer not to do so because I don't find contacting them useful in solving the problem . . . . I don't know if they received my emails . . . . you don't know if they will contact you back." India2

Q. Is it difficult to shop online with Western companies?

"Yes, [I shop online] almost every week. If there is nothing else to do and I get online and shop online . . . . [but] I don't usually shop a lot on Western online companies; we have middle [seller] who can browse things overseas, like Prada and Gucci. We can buy through them. It is a lot cheaper than buying from China. If we want makeup or something we contact those sellers and they buy the Western products for us. There is a trust factor to allow the seller to help guide the sale than to allow the Western company to deliver the product. When we get a problem with the products the seller will not help us contact the company. I don't think the sellers have licenses . . . . so it depends on the trust between the customer and the seller. I think when we get problems with the product the seller will not help us contact the Western company, that is one of the things they tell us. The sellers are overseas, like in the United States and Britain. We cannot contact them very frequently and if we want to change or return the product we have to contact the United States directly. So that is a complex thing for us so I don't think the customer wants to do that once they get a product. They will not complain about the product. We don't shop directly also because a lot of companies cannot be reached because our Internet is kind of blocked. That is one [main] reason. I think a lot of Western companies like Gucci or Prada, those companies cannot mail the things internationally. They can only mail it in the United States or Britain. . . . But if you want to buy it in China maybe they have the website for Chinese people but we are concerned about the price because

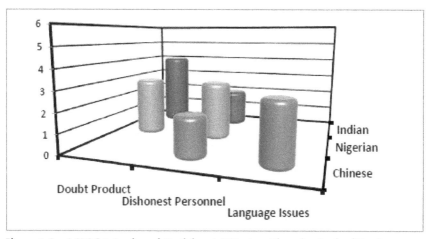

Figure 4.6.   NWFC Interviewed Participants' Western Shopping Lack of Trust
Created by Chizoma C. Nosiri

the price is much more expensive so a lot of people prefer to buy it through the agents." China3

"I know a few people that have complained that the items that they see online when they see it physically it is not exactly the way it is presented online. . . . Returning things is difficult online." Nigeria2

"Online [personnel] cannot do anything other than deliver the product. They tell you that you have to deal with the company that makes it. [For example] if I buy an Apple product and I get the laptop or phone through Amazon, if there is a problem in the product I have to contact Apple not Amazon." India3

". . . [Indians] don't trust that if you order your money will be drafted from your card and they are not sure whether you would be getting that product or not since your money had been deducted from your card. With a local company you are getting the product right away and you are paying them right away. [Also] just being there with the local company, you could just give [the product] a try without ordering a huge bottle online. [Also there is website hosting concerns]. We don't know if it is an authentic company or not." India5

Theme: Historically and Globally Not Being Heard/Understood

Although the majority of the NWFC interview participants believed in self-expressing their concerns in a proactive and confident manner, some of the NWFCs expressed difficulty in doing so. The participants admitted that they had concerns of communication pathways and expression channels which prevented them from expressing their concerns as they would like. Although Nigeria4 expressed that contacting the Western corporation to express her concern is an irritation for her, "No, I will not contact them because I would not like to bother myself or bother the company," the remaining NWFCs had major communication structure concerns. Several of the NWFCs stated that, they had significant problems with contacting Western corporations because of not being heard or understand.

Q. Have you ever been treated unfairly or badly by a Western company?

(As stated previously in "Lack of Trust" theme) "I feel like some of the Western companies discriminate. They can tell that my English is different . . . " China1

"Online email is the best contact method for me. I just don't like to deal with waiting for them to email me or forwarding my email from person to person." China5

"Truly, I feel like it is going to be a waste of my time. Yeah, I feel like I am going to make all these calls to the foreign company and they'll be like, 'Hold on, you can talk to my "Oga" my supervisor' who says, 'We'll make a decision at the office. We'll get back to you.' Two days, three days, four days, later you call again and you have to explain yourself all over again, and nobody is really listening. You spend your airtime because there are no free calls and you get really angry and frustrated and in the end you don't even get to return it, so we don't even bother." Nigeria2

Theme: Conflict Avoidance, Unfamiliarity and Being Seen as the "Other"

Seven out of the eighteen NWFC interview participants expressed that they would avoid conflict if they contacted the Western company and got a negative response. Knowing that conflict could be present while expressing their concerns, many of those who were sensitive to conflict took precaution to reduce it by either approaching Western corporations through polite language, preferred the emailing method in order to avoid phone interactions, and some simply stopped shopping with the Western corporations.

Q. How do you react to conflict?

"Personally, I'm kind of like the conflict avoidance people. I don't like to have a fight or quarrel with someone. I want to be polite. I think that if you are polite people are more likely to help you out." China3

"[That's why] I prefer Western emailing system. . . . I don't have to see the person face-to-face and I am able to talk about the problem through email and then get the problem fixed through email." China5

"I'm free to say what I feel online. I would rather talk to foreign companies' personnel online than talk to native businesses' personnel in my country. I just like not having conflict face-to-face [so] I don't talk too much about the situation and try to just move on" Nigeria5

"When you have a problem with the company you call them but it depends if the company has a warrantee, if they don't have a warrantee you cannot call them [and complain]" Nigeria6

"For me if [the product] gets delayed or they don't answer properly then obviously I will get irritated and pissed off. If they don't answer properly then I don't want to call, that attitude might come, then I keep away from them" India3

Q. What are some ways you avoid conflict with a Western company when you are dissatisfied with their services or their products?

"If I don't like [the product] they change it. If they don't agree with me I don't talk to them again." China2

"I don't mind conflict but I don't like having to talk to foreign companies about their products over and over again. I just leave it alone." India2

Theme: Individual Marketplace Strength/Collectivistic Approach

Most of the NWFC interviewed participants would tell their family and friends about their bad experiences with Western corporations, however, their first initial focus and action was to contact the Western corporation before speaking about the situation with others. Some of the NWFC interview participants would complain to friends and family while they contact the Western corporation. Most of the NWFCs preferred to speak to the Western corporations before relaying any message about the Western corporation to family and friends (See Figure 4.7). They believed it was important to share with the Western corporation before informing others.

Q. When you received bad service or a bad product from Western companies did you tell your family and friends about it?

"If I was having a problem and my friends just happen to be around me before I called the company I would definitely talk to them." China3

"Yes, yes, yes. If there is a product that I used that didn't work or was not good, I would definitely tell my friends. . . . I don't want them to have the same experience." Nigeria2

"Yes, I would share my experience with my family and friends . . . but ultimately I will talk to the company . . . ." India6

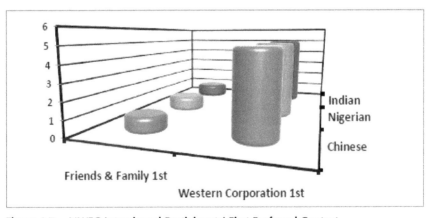

Figure 4.7. NWFC Interviewed Participants' First Preferred Contact
Created by Chizoma C. Nosiri

Q. When you received bad service or a bad product do you contact the Western company first or tell your family and friends first?

> "No, I don't [talk about it with my friends and family]. I will solve them by myself. I don't like to talk about them with my family." China6

> "I think contacting them first is better. I would call the company first before talking to my family and friends." Nigeria1

> "I would call the Western company first. But if the company continues to not help me then I might talk to my family and friends, they would understand." Nigeria3

Theme: Online vs. Local

Although many of the NWFC interview participants preferred to shop locally and in-person, all of the NWFCs expressed a desire for better local native businesses' customer return services (See Figure 4.8). Some believed that Western corporations were more pleasant to talk to than local native businesses. India6 asserted that, "Western companies are more customer-friendly." This local native business concern made the NWFCs desire a pro-Western structure of online customer service approach for local purchases. With restrictions like English, high-context culture norms (i.e. in-person and personal familiarity with store owners) and risk acquired by shopping for products that were not physically examined, each of the NWFCs asserted that Western corporations had issues that prevented them from expressing their concerns online. A few NWFC interview participants worried about foreign shipping expense, China5 explained, "The transportation fee is expensive with Western companies but if they have a store here then it is fine."

Online Preferred:

Q. Do you find it difficult to express your concerns when you contact local native businesses?

> "No, but I like the online shopping approach. I shop on Alibaba and other Asian stores. I go to Amazon and other foreign companies too. I don't know local companies have sales but on the Internet, I can know it easily. I prefer online, however, it is difficult to communicate unless they have a Chinese site." China1

> "In walk-in shops they do not take items back. You can only look at it [during the time of purchase] and say 'I don't want this.' There are so many stores that just don't take it back [after you leave the store with the item]." Nigeria2

> "Online I am able to get what I want without waiting for others in a line. [Although] I can return things locally but that is not easy to do so, it depends on your relationship with the manager." Nigeria3

"As far as the Indian market is concern, they never really help you. Once they identify the problem with the product they still don't response positively. With foreign companies they . . . respond better to complaints. They respond positively, I think so." India1

Q. Do you contact local companies if you have a problem or a concern with their service or need to return a product?

"I think that the return policy is much better with Western companies than in China. Returning things in China is not very easy for me. If I want to return, the people say things like 'I think you are already wearing that you cannot return that stuff.' But with Western companies [Amazon], as long as I give the reason like the size does not fit me, then that is alright. In China the policy is thirty days after you buy but after one or two weeks it would be hard to return something." China3

"Talking is easier [locally] but American companies have better customer services. In China they are not use to dealing with exchanges or conflict. For example, if I have to exchange something Chinese companies do not help, they say you already bought it." China4

"It is not the same. Sometimes you don't get the response you want immediately. . . . Maybe by the time you go and come back they are out of the stuff. They may give you an option but it is not what you wanted or need. . . . I would prefer expressing my concerns online [with Western companies]." Nigeria1

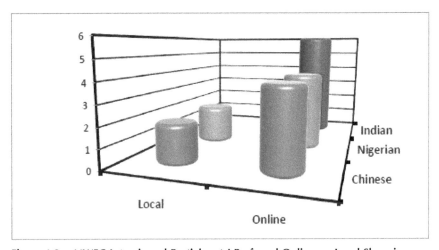

Figure 4.8. NWFC Interviewed Participants' Preferred Online vs. Local Shopping
Created by Chizoma C. Nosiri

Local Preferred:

Q. Do you find it difficult to express your concerns when you contact local native businesses?

"I like local companies better. They are here. . . . If I buy from Internet it is convenient but there are risks." China2

"The advantage is I can communicate freely with [the local company] because my oral English is not good. I want to communicate with local company." China6

"The direct market is better because you see the customer one-on-one [in-person] and you see the quality of the product. You see the product and the price is right there." Nigeria3

"At times the local company services are better than Western company services when I complain. They know me better." Nigeria4

LANGUAGE BARRIER

Theme: English Language Domination

The Nigerian NWFC interview participants believed that speaking English was convenient but writing in English posed a problem for most of them. With only the exception of Nigeria5, "I'm ok writing English text. That's not a concern for me," the interviewed Nigerian women believed that most Nigerians would have a problem writing in English, and they prefer to talk in English. The Indian NWFCs also desired to speak in English than write their concerns on an email. India2 stated, "I would not contact foreign companies on their online tools even if I was allowed to speak in my native language," reflecting the discomfort to communicate by email and also expressing a concern of her inability to speak English fluently. All of the NWFC Chinese interviewees had a problem speaking English (See Figure 4.9).

English is not a problem:

Q. Do you feel that English is a problem when expressing your concerns?

"Yes, for many people in Nigeria . . . English is the 'lingua franca' so everybody speaks their native language but in every school foundation is English. . . . But a whole lot of people may not be able to communicate effectively, like in writing or typing. And a whole lot of people speak pidgin . . . you know, broken English, it's like English but you're not actually communicating properly. No, it's not a problem for me. But I think it's a problem for many people. I work in a bank and for five years I worked in customer services. There are a lot of people who have problems that come to the bank and they want to complain a lot and when I say, 'We need to put this information down in writing so when meetings come up and if we need to refer to stuff like that and they say, 'Oh no no no, that's ok.' It's even bad enough where there was a customer that was being defrauded by a bank staff member and I told her if she does put it down in writing I can't take it up with the bank executives and she didn't want to write it down. A lot of people here in Nigeria are like that. They would rather not write or write things down on their own." Nigeria2

"Now people are familiar communicating in English, so it would be easy. . . . Some phrases may not be what I feel that I would like to use it correctly from the different perception. Being a Nepal Indian woman, I may perceive it differently and the person who is reading that email may perceive it differently. Most of the women from urban areas would be able to communicate and are smart enough to do with typing English, but in remote areas it would be hard to do." India5

English is a problem:

Q. Do you feel that English is a problem when expressing your concerns?

"Yes, I can talk to Amazon by email in Chinese [Mandarin]. I don't have to talk in English, so it's easy. That is the only type of Western company I email. They must be in Chinese. My English is not very good, so I often choose Chinese companies. If I see something on a Western online site that I really have to have I use procurement service, I ask other people [to] buy it for me. It is difficult to buy from Western companies [who are English based only] because I go through a third party, and it becomes a big hassle and returning is difficult." China1

Q. Do you feel like you are confidence enough to call and speak up?

"No, I think I have language barrier when I talk to Western companies. So maybe I would say I am fifty percent confident and I have worry. I think, 'Can I just tell them what I want or will I make mistake. Will I offend them or not.' I worry about it. So I email them. I can make sure of what I am saying. Yes, I have felt that [intimidation]. I try to make sure I am right before I contact them. It is difficult to be really confident. The language barrier is difficult and my ability to talk to them is not enough. . . . Most Chinese have a problem talking in English. In Chinese there are more and more people who want to shop from foreign countries especially from America because it is cheaper and they can avoid taxes. . . . I watched this TV program and saw that there are lectures on how to shop from American companies online because they don't know English and they don't know how the credit cards works, or how the shipping and management of problems [conflict] works. So I heard that so many people are interested in these lectures. They attend these lectures to learn about how to shop in American online sites. English is a big problem. I lived in America for over 5 years before coming back home but still I have hard time. . . . I also have a hard time writing chatting with them. So I think that language barriers are very big problem." China1

Q. Do you believe that not knowing English well diminished your voice in expressing yourself to Western companies?

"Yes. I think so. That is a big problem. Even for me, I prefer to chat online than to call customer services. I don't directly call them because sometimes I cannot explain a lot of problems very clearly. It is just complicated and some-times the cannot understand me very clearly and sometimes I cannot under-stand them . . . .so I prefer to type online. But if you were to ask me the order for contacting Western companies I would prefer to chat online first and then emailing them because it takes forever to hear back from them. I think that for Asian people sometimes we don't like to contact foreigners . . . . I do think it is a little bit a culture things because the agents are Chinese people. So like, for example if my Mom wants to buy something she would prefer to talk to the agent. She can talk to the agent with Chinese. That would be better because they would understand because we share the same culture background. So we understand what they are talking about and what we want. If there is problem we can talk to the agent that may be easier for them when it comes to customer service than to talk to a Westerner." China3

"I think it is hard. Maybe now, you hear me as I try to talk to you . . . a language problem is there and I can try to talk to them through the Internet but it is hard because the phone is best. I want to talk on the phone but not on email." India1

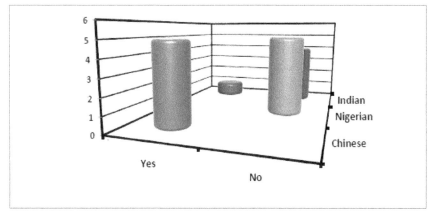

Figure 4.9. NWFC Interviewed Participants' English Barrier Restriction
Created by Chizoma C. Nosiri

SOCIAL MEDIA WORD-OF-MOUTH COMMUNICATION

Theme: Social Media Cultural Clash and A Collectivistic Loyalty Approach

Collectivistic culture approach was a theme derived through the actions and behaviors associated through the NWFCs response to utilizing social media to talk about their concerns with Western corporations. China4 asserted that she shares her concerns on a Chinese blog where people would share information about all Western companies in China "like Target, Walmart and everything." Nigeria6 asserted that, "the only people that can handle my problem are the consumer services. So, if they have a company's WhatsApp website she would contact them there." The remaining sixteen NWFC interviewees were against expressing their concerns through social media sites and believed in protecting the Western corporations by not bad mouthing them; others felt that it would not solve their problems (See Figure 4.10).

Q. Do you think the online social media approach to express your opinion is a more convenient way to address your concerns than having Western computer-mediated communication tools?

> "No, I often use QQ in China. It's a social media site [or] Weixin it's like Face-book [but] I don't say my complaints there. I don't want to talk about a company on the Internet. It's bad to talk about a company online. I complain to my friends and family face-to-face." China1

> "You only should communicate with them through their website not through social media. I would complain to my friends and the company at the same time but I would never complain on social media." China2

> "I do not use social media to generalize the online word-of-mouth . . . because I am not the kind of person to share everything in my life online, I don't like to tweet or Facebook about everything happening in my life so I would not do that." China3

> "I try to fix the problem with the company by contacting them. If I cannot make the changes, I think it is personal and I think about the company's image. So if I can't get it fix I talk to my friends and feel better." China4

> "No, I would not say anything on social media. I would not go there. I would not bother. I would just call the customer services directly. I would not complain on social media. I don't think it is helpful when you see people ranting about companies online." Nigeria2

> "I would never talk about the company online through Facebook. I would talk to my family about the situation but first the company." Nigeria4

"No, I would not talk bad about them online. I'm not a bully. I don't like to spend time on such things. I spent my time on good things." India1

"I would never talk about the foreign company online or on social media; it is not the best way. I don't believe that talking bad about them on social media is the right thing to do." India2

"It would be better to contact the company to get the right answer why I got that consequence and so on. Just talking to the third person does not fix my problem. If I want to fix my problem I need to communicate with the company so they would know what I want and I know their expectations. It is like a visa-versa [working with them]." India5

Q. Which would you rather use to express your concern about a Western company, the Western company's online tool or social media (Facebook, Twitter, etc.)?

"No. I never use Facebook or any other social media platform to talk about the companies. . . . I don't feel comfortable sharing my opinions with people I don't know. It is not useful and it could take their customers away. I would contact them instead of the whole world." China5

"For me I would not do that. No, it is better to contact them directly because you do not want to spoil their customers and tarnish their character on social media because a lot of people go there, by seeing that people will not buy from them . . . a lot of people will make comments about it and you're making them lose a lot of customers." Nigeria1

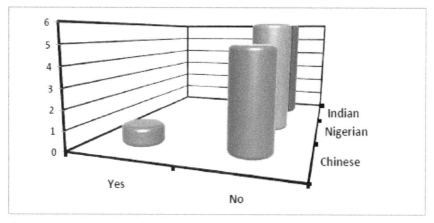

Figure 4.10. NWFC Interviewed Participants' Social Media Word-of-Mouth Usage
Created by Chizoma C. Nosiri

"I would like to call the company myself. Anytime I have a problem I call them instead of talk about them on Facebook. It is good to hear from the company and I am their customer." Nigeria3

"I would not express it on social media. The company's tool is the best way to send the message to the foreign company . . . so they have to know what is happening with their product." Nigeria5

"Not really. Facebook has become bigger groups, we have too many friends where you don't know who knows the problem or who does not, whether they need information or not, so it's a lot of things. So we have WhatsApp, a group chatting with a group of 10 to 15 members. We can chat instead of telling ten thousand people. If the service is bad we should complain but we can't particularly tell others that the product is bad and we should ban it and discourage people from buying from the company." India3

Chapter Five

Discussion

INTRODUCTION

As previously explained in the Non-Western female consumer (NWFC) result findings in Chapter 4, the purpose of this study was to explore the influence of self-confidence, cultural norms and language barriers in diminishing the NWFC's expression when communicating her concerns to Western corporations through their computer-mediated communication (CMC) tools. By understanding the NWFC's perspective and behavior in approaching the Western corporations and her ability to express her concerns utilizing Western corporation's online communication tools, research question number one was answered.

SELF-CONFIDENCE AND COMPLAINTS

RQ1. Does lack of self-confidence diminish the Non-Western female consumer's voice in expressing her concerns to Western corporations through their computer-mediated communication tools?

Proactive Communication Confidence (Self-Efficacy and Ability): A centered issue for NWFC participant group.

Productivity and high confidence was not a lacking attribute for the NWFC interview participants. As the exploration revealed, it is evident that the NWFC interview participants were confident and had a desire to express their concerns and were overall confident in expressing their concerns during conflict. The meaning within the experience illustrated that when conflictual situations arises the NWFC interview participants were proactive in expressing their thoughts and would do so with Western corporations if they had the opportunity. Three major factors that influence the NWFC interview participants to embrace a proactive communication confidence were (1) cultural norms; (2) collectivistic culture; and (3) modernity.

CULTURAL NORMS

In regards to the NWFC interview participants, expressing their concerns is a normal part of shopping for them and a way of asserting their consumer rights. The NWFC interviewed participants' assertiveness and strength was visible in their quest to assert themselves to Western corporations. They were eager to be recognized and heard. In addition, cultural upbringing and market strategies to sale and trade goods within marketplaces and consumer situations (Sudarkasa, 1996; Agarwal, 1997; Fan, 2003) prevent many of them from being submissive and powerless in the market environment which they historically have dominated (Oyewumi, 2002; Dong & Li, 2007).

The NWFC interview participants' proactive, expressive and self-confident characteristic discredits the "muted" group (Ardener, 1978) assumption of Western observers. The "muted" assumption is contradictory to the NWFC true characteristics. In addition, Nai Li and Gill Kirkup's 2007 investigation promotes a notion that Chinese females (as well as other Non-Western females) have less confidence in their abilities to use computers and the Internet. Such studies are limited in addressing the online marketplace environment (Chinese female students shopping on Amazon and emailing Amazon about their concerns) and the English language barrier (which limits self-efficacy and determines what online language platform they use). Such studies cannot address the self-confidence of Chinese females in the context of online consumerism or their proactive confidence engagement in computer and Internet usages.

COLLECTIVIST CULTURE

The reason behind the NWFC interview participants' high confidence and interaction to voice their concerns and complaints to unsatisfying Western corporations was their proactive involvement which they also viewed as a consumer's responsibility. They believe in informing the corporations or businesses they buy from, whether Western or local, about their dissatisfaction, concerns, or faults with products and services. This action and behavior is known as "face-saving" (DeVito, 2010; Beebe & Ivy, 2012), a strategy and attribute of the collectivist culture. The collectivist culture controls crisis situations by providing their opponent a face saving way out of the crisis. Understanding the value of the corporations' social status, the NWFC interview participants have the desire to assist the corporations from "losing face" (Beebe & Ivy, 2012). They help the corporations sustain corporate esteem when they might otherwise be embarrassed. The NWFC interview participants seek to preserve the corporations' reputation and credibility. The collectivistic face-saving strategy shows care that builds both trust and obligation for Western corporations by the NWFC interview participants, which they expect to be reciprocal. Furthermore, this collectivist approach utilized by the NWFC interview participants builds loyalty with Western corporations, however, hinders the NWFC local collectivist culture agenda (i.e. word-of-mouth with family and friends).

MODERNITY

Culture is not stagnant. It is continuously changing (DeVito, 2010). Since culture is changing with global interventions, a renunciation of the past, desiring a new beginning, and a re-interpretation and innovative movements impose modernity (Toulmin, 1992). The NWFC interview participants are keepers of their culture, however, a slow change of culture facilitated by online "transnational cultural construction" (Gilroy, 1993) is brewing. The connection of the NWFCs' local birth place and the new found CMC virtual space creates an empowering blend (Hongladarom, 1999; Ahmed & Kokil, 2013) prompting expression (Katz's, 1959) for the NWFC interview participants on a global environment.

Modernity does not have to be Westernization or globally infused, and modernity key processes and dynamics are found in all societies (Delanty, 2007). Similar to the denotation of the word "model," as in an individual who displays fashion, modernity can be reflected as the fashion of civilizations, cultures, and societies, required by the flow of time and change to refashion itself. As a move to modernize expression, the NWFC interview participants are gaining more skills in workplaces, control of the economic market globally with technology, and intellectually are becoming empowered to express their concerns, inequalities of gender discrimination (Agarwal, 2003; McPhail, 2010; Kevin MacDonald, 2010).

Although all the NWFC interview participants were confident when approached with opportunities during conflict in expressing and interacting with Western corporations, their eagerness to self-express never diminished, yet their ability to do so diminished due to the Western corporations' CMC platforms of communication which does not cater to the NWFC interviewed participants cultural norms and language structure. Although the NWFC interview participants are not silent, the structures of Western corporations' CMC tools diminish her voice and promote a discourse of "muteness" by Western observers (Ardener, 1975).

CULTURE AND CONFLICT

In exploring the self-efficacy and ability of the NWFC interview participants in expressing their concerns, it was recognized that communication platforms, language barriers, and the impact of their local culture environment, compared to existing in the new virtual environment influences the NWFC interview participants' behaviors and actions. By understanding the NWFC interview participants' perspective and the role culture plays in their attempt to resolve difficulties and conflict with Western corporations through the corporations' online tools, research question number two was answered.

RQ2. How do cultural differences diminish the Non-Western female consumer's voice in expressing her concerns to Western corporations through their computer-mediated communication tools?

Cultural Clash and High Context Culture: Eagerness to express without conflict intenseness and barriers and a need to connect.

As most Western corporations are unreachable to Chinese society, the Chinese NWFC interview participants were further limited in their ability to express concerns. This created unfamiliarity with Western corporations (Lim, 2010). It also caused the Chinese NWFC interview participants to feel a sense of disengagement with Western corporations. The Nigeria and India NWFC interview participants were equally eager to speak about the concerns to Western corporations. The Nigerian and Indian NWFC interview participants' cultures have high use of non-verbal elements (paralinguistics and kinetics) such as facial expression, eye contact, voice tone, body movements, and gestures which carry significant parts of conversation for high-context cultures. Verbal message is implicit since context (i.e. people, nonverbal elements and the situation) is more significant than words (i.e. text). The NWFC interview participants' cultures focus on communication as an art form and a way to engage others in order to truly hear, understand the speaker and take them seriously. With the virtual environment clashing with their high-context culture, the NWFC interview participants' inability to hear and listen for the voice tones of the speaker made it difficult for them to communicate their concerns with the Western corporations on their customer online tools.

Not having in-person communication created uneasiness and anxiety (Kanter, 2005) for the NWFC interview participants. In addition, communicating on the online sphere which is an unfamiliar territory (McIlroy, Bunting, Tierney, & Gordon, 2001) for expression left most of the NWFC interview participants with the phone conversation as the second best alternative. Hence, most of the NWFC interview participants' virtual existence, from their basic survival in self-expression needs to self-fulfillment needs (Maslow, 1987; Lim, 2010), clashes with their ability to express themselves in the manner they are most familiar with. As described by Maslow's Hierarchy of Needs Theory applied to virtual existence, if one does not have this sense of belonging (Katz, 1959), the next stages above "esteem" (confidence), and self-actualization in Maslow's "Hierarchy of Needs" are unreachable. The NWFC interview participants' unfamiliarity and discomfort with the Western email tools (Katz, 1959; Fusilier, Durlabhji, Cucchi, & Collins, 2005; Joseph, 2013) results in their desire to express their concerns by phone. Unfortunately, in their attempt to speak by the phone platform, they encountered lengthy waiting periods as they reach out to connect with Western personnel, long distance calling costs, which created negative experiences for some and a lack of trust to have concerns resolved.

Lack of Trust and Not Being Heard or Understood: Diminishing the NWFCs ability to engage in online consumerism and complaints without doubts.

The Nigerian and Indian NWFC interview participants who preferred the email method favored it because it allowed them to complete their thought expression and their desire to have a paper trial of their conversation with the Western corporations. However, the main reason was that some of them had a lack of trust in speaking with Western corporations by phone because of their past experiences of not being heard or transferred from one Western personnel to another. On the other hand, the Nigerian and Indian NWFC interview participants who utilized the email method were also doubtful that their emails would be answered, which created "feedback" concern (Katz, 1959) that their expressions and concerns (their voices) and status (value, courage, confidence, and empowerment) would not be acknowledged (Katz, 1959).These concerns illustrate the "otherness" felt by the NWFC interview participants (Lugones, 1987; Alcoff, 1991; Jaggar, 1998).

The NWFC interview participants' experience with Western corporations created a distance to trust that they were being taken seriously during phone complaints and hopelessness of resolution for their concerns.

While some Nigerian and Indian NWFC interview participants did not trust Western corporations websites, others were concerned about delivery of the products since they were unable to examine the products in-person and physically. Other NWFC interview participants were concerned that they were not taken seriously when they called Western corporations. From insecurity of websites, local environment precautions (such as not returning items so they don't alert their interactions with Western corporations to local thieves) to keeping evidence of their actions and responses from Western corporations as they navigated in an environment (Aderemi et al., 2008), the unfamiliarity of the online sphere promotes a vulnerable dependency that triggers an inability to perform complaint expression tasks. The lack of competence in technology and habitual cultural norms of product evaluation and consumer expression (Oyewumi, 2002) during purchases diminishes the NWFC interview participants' voices. Utilizing Maslow's Hierarchy of Needs Theory, these obstacles fit into the "physiological" stage or the "safety" stage (Lim, 2010). In this instance, existing online (breathing and security) is a necessity and feeling unsafe in online purchases and complaint responses limits expression for the NWFC interview participants.

Individual Marketplace Strength/Collectivistic Approach: The NWFC's power of loyalty and working together.

During conflict, the majority of the NWFC interview participants disagreed with informing their family and friends about the situation. They were more eager to express their concerns to the Western corporations. Although some informed family and friends as they contacted the Western corporations simultaneously, the main focus was on addressing the Western corporations. This loyalty to inform the Western corporations prompts a lack of negative word-of-mouth (WOM) from the NWFC interview participants and forms a loyalty characteristic. Although this stance to present the NWFC interview participants as "silent" (Ardener, 1975) in expressing concern on social media sites, or to family and friends is a usual formality for collectivistic culture (DeVito, 2010), it historically justified the strength and independency of the NWFC as marketplace dominators, with an individual marketplace strength (Sudarkasa, 1996; Agarwal, 1997; Fan, 2003), collectivistic approach, face-saving loyalty attribute (Beebe & Ivy, 2012) (refraining from negative WOM on social media and locally), and hopefulness for connection, belonging (Katz, 1959; Maslow, 1987; Lim, 2010), validation and return of acceptance in the virtual world. Moving forward, the NWFC interview participants' lack of ability to express their concerns through Western corporations CMC tools may frustrate them in their future Western online purchases and force the NWFC interview participants to disengagement from expressing frustrations to Western corporations and engage in negative WOM expression.

Conflict Avoidance and Online vs. Local: An ideal cultural blend suited for the NWFC.

As the exploration revealed, the Chinese NWFC interview participants' high-context culture of in-person interaction and experiences along with Chinese corporate personnel negative reactions to their expressed concerns were influential to their preferred expression platform, which was the corporate online tools. The cultural ways, values, lifestyles (Machin & Mayr, 2012) of the Chinese NWFC interview participants also promoted them to seek a less conflicting expression format that will allow them to express themselves without interruption. Although communicating in-person was preferred by the Nigerian and Indian NWFC interview participants, the experience the participants have had locally prompted a preference for Western return policies format within an in-person interactions. A blend of the two is classified as a homogenization of the local cultures to the global Western environment (Hongladarom, 1999; Gilroy, 1993) bringing together the best of the two cultures and merging them into an ideal approach that can cater to NWFC interview participants.

Being habitually normalized to a collectivistic culture (DeVito, 2010), the NWFC interview participants were against pursuing conflict after their first initial complaint to the corporations and businesses, both Western and local. In regards to Western corporations, the NWFC interview participants simply would not contact the corporations after their initial communication with them since the product was bought online (Aderemi et al., 2008). Culturally, the NWFC interview participants do not like to deal with negative communication situations that escalate but instead desire to solve the problem by saving face for both parties (Beebe & Ivy, 2012). Instead, the NWFC interview participants would stop the increasing conflict quickly and resolute to stop shopping with the Western corporations in the future or shop less online altogether.

Culture influenced the desire to decrease conflict for the NWFC interview participants. This also diminished their expression of concern in order to continue to exist (Lim, 2010) as online shoppers instead of disengaging on online shopping. This embraces the notion that for collectivistic individuals to function in an unfamiliar world such as the virtual world they would need to become more bicultural since it is necessary to communicate and function in a multicultural environment (Yamada & Singelis, 1999). This effect influences the NWFC interview participants to limit their expressive characteristics in order to continue to take advantage of the online shopping environment that Western corporations offer. This portrays the NWFC interview participants as "mute" individuals (Ardener, 1975) although they are merely fitting in as a choice to continue engaging in online shopping rather than a necessity to be involved in the online world.

ENGLISH LANGUAGE DOMINATION

The NWFC interview participants were able to express in detail the ways in which they communicate in order to express their concerns when they are is confronted by language barrier obstacles. In addition, allowing the NWFC interview participants to speak through in-depth interviewing, the NWFC interview participants verified the impact that language barriers has on their ability to express their concerns to Western corporations, thereby answering research question number three.

RQ3. How do language barriers diminish the Non-Western female consumer's voice in expressing her concerns to Western corporations through their computer-mediated communication tools?

Language Barrier: Restricting the NWFC expression and connection to Western corporations.

Another battle that the NWFC interview participants encountered was the English language. The Nigerian and Indian NWFC interview participants voiced their concerns on how the English language influences their behavior in expressing their concerns and the limitation of expression by other individuals within their country because of their lack of ability to speak or write in English. English impacted the Chinese NWFC interview participants the most. The Chinese NWFC interview participants were confident and eager to express their concerns, however, their high-context culture (i.e., in-person interaction phone conversation) was unachievable because of the English language barrier (Ye, 2005) that restricted them from communicating to Western corporations' personnel and forced them to distance themselves from expressing their concerns and communicating with Western corporations by phone. The need to express their concerns was then accomplished through the means of emailing. The email platform assisted to break the English language barrier. It allowed the Chinese NWFC interview participants to communicate their concerns without interruption. As illustrated by Katz's (1959) Uses and

Gratification Theory first need, which is the affective needs (i.e. emotion and feelings), the emailing platform allowed the Chinese NWFC interview participants a voice to express and vent "negative feelings" about their corporate complaints and concerns online.

Language creates existence (Wodak & Mayer, 2009) and the English language must be an established language to communicate with Western corporations that do not cater to Chinese customers who can't speak English. Unfortunately, the difficulty of shopping on English dominated sites created a struggle for the Chinese NWFC interview participants' complaint behavior and a sense of lack of belonging for them. As explained by Katz's (1959) Uses and Gratification Theory second need which is personal integrative needs (credibility, stability, and status), a "recognition" to belong and not feel disassociated and unwelcomed is relevant in promoting healthy connections on the virtual environment. In addition, the ban on Western sites made it even more difficult for Chinese NWFC interview participants to shop with Western corporations. This prompted the Chinese NWFC interview participants to shop for Western products through procurement services with limited expression of concerns and dissatisfaction even further.

The procurement services created an even greater gap in communication and connection in expressing concerns and complaint for the Chinese NWFC interview participants. This lack of connection between the Western corporations and the Chinese NWFC interview participants created a cultural clash. It also prevented interaction and resolution of the NWFC interview participants' complaint concerns. In addition, the procurement services further diminished the Chinese NWFC interview participants' ability return products and establish corporation loyalty.

A couple of the Indian and Nigerian NWFC interview participants had difficulties speaking English, however, the European colonization of India (Robin, 2003) and Nigeria (Harris, 2013) promoted the English language. Hence, almost all of the Nigerian and Indian NWFC interview participants were able to express their concerns in English by text or by phone. Although all of the Nigerian and Indian NWFC interview participants were able to communicate in English enough to express their concerns by email or phone, the cultural clash of their high-context culture (DeVito, 2010) restricted their use all CMC platform methods.

SOCIAL MEDIA WORD-OF-MOUTH COMMUNICATION

In exploring the role culture plays in the NWFC interview participants' compliant behavior and strategies, an understanding of the outcomes of culture and the discourse it creates is visible. Although labeled as "mute" by many Western observers, in this study the NWFC interview participants expressed and explained their (Western assumed "mute") behavior and voiced their perspective. By allowing the NWFC interview participants to speak through in-depth interviewing, the NWFC interview participants verified the motives in their behavior and the factors that distance them from expressing their concerns to Western corporations, not only through corporate customer service tools but through social media platforms, thereby answering research question number four.

RQ4. Have social media platforms changed the Non-Western female consumer's complaint behavior and her actions in expressing her concerns through other venues?

Social Media Cultural Clash and A Collectivistic Approach: Face-saving is the ultimate loyalty of the NWFC and connecting glue to gaining their favor.

Katz's (1959) Uses and Gratification Theory third need which is social integrative needs (i.e. web-sphere chat rooms) may give the NWFC interview participants the ability to connect socially and create a safe haven for growth on computer-mediated communication social media platforms. These platforms are contrary to the collectivistic culture approach. All of the NWFC interview participants in the study were against using social media to discuss their concerns about Western corporations to the mass users of social media (Groundswell, 2011). Although one NWFC interview participant stated that she would discuss her concern on a social media group and another stated that she would direct her concerns with the Western corporations on their social media site, it was evident that the NWFC interview participants were strongly culturally collectivistic in their approach.

The face-saving collectivistic cultural approach (Beebe & Ivy, 2012; Zhang, van Doorn & Leeflang, 2018) allowed them to avoid or compromise in resolving their complaints with Western corporations. Face-saving can be active or passive. In active face-saving, individuals help and rescue others (i.e. taking the blame for things that are not your fault). In passive face-saving individuals avoid actions that would embarrass the other individual, or in this case the corporations. Embarrassing the corporations is to insult them and challenge them to conflict (DeVito, 2010). In this regard, the NWFC interview participants engaged in active face-saving to assist the corporations in passive face-saving to avoid increasing conflict.

Chapter Six

Resolutions, Recommendations, Conclusion

INTRODUCTION

A global village is inevitable, and the Non-Western female consumer (NWFC) and Western corporations should be able to live in it harmoniously. This study indicates that the NWFC and Western corporations have tremendous work to do in order to resolve the disconnection and cultural communication barriers that exists between them if there is to be a successful virtual sphere that caters to Non-Western female consumership. This research debunks the "mute" assumptions that may be prevalent in scholarship and assumed "muteness" of the NWFC in the visual world. Furthermore, this research found loopholes in Li and Kirkup's 2007 investigation which generalizes self-confidence in computer use without evaluating the context of difference situations (i.e. the web market-sphere and language barriers) that determine self-efficacy of Chinese females. In addition, this study is a resolution tool for the NWFC to utilize and work on the appropriate themes that may diminish and disempowers her voice. As most of the NWFC interview participants noted, their self-efficacy is high but the virtual execution platforms are limited. However, the NWFC interview participants recognize the value of the online consumer environment and the advantages that it offers them.

A STRONG FEMALE VOICE FINALLY HEARD

Once the NWFC is able to break free from the barriers that prevent her from expressing her concerns to Western corporations, she can find comfort, belonging, and claim a healthy existence within the virtual world. For example, if themes such as "lack of trust" and "social media cultural clash" are eliminated or transformed by the NWFC into an exploration experience in understanding the virtual world and propelling online consumer activism, she still can keep her collectivistic culture intact by expressing complaints in helpful rhetoric and politeness on Western corporation's social media tools. The NWFC should (1) remove her "otherness" by familiarizing herself with the virtual world's consumer sphere and media security (i.e. class on media literacy); (2) collectively work together with other local native females to empower each other to continue to express concerns to Western corporations; and (3) continually express her concerns, engage in, and be involved in consumerism both locally and globally to intertwine and blend the two worlds in ways that empower her shopping ability and power. These strategies will provide the NWFC a proactive stance in determining the future of international consumer relations and recognition as an active online consumer, hence, changing the discourse of the NWFC consumer voice and (re)presenting her as she truly is, strong and proactive.

Change depends not only on the NWFC, but more so on Western corporations. The NWFC's lack of expression concerns and communication limitations to Western corporations are mainly caused by Western corporations' assumptions of "muteness" of the NWFC, and creations and dominating variables (i.e. English language domination, email online contact platform). As the NWFC is plagued by obstacles that diminish her voice which are mainly constructed by Western corporations' communication platforms, it becomes obvious to her that the Western corporations' customer initiatives do not cater to her. The NWFC's cultural norm is to be proactive but Western barriers prompt her to disengage continuously from confronting Western corporations. This fosters an assumption of invisibility of the NWFC on the international market and online sphere. These Western barriers make it almost impossible for her to be recognized and prevent her proactive consumer involvement stance in the virtual world.

The need for Western corporations to assist to lift the NWFC whose voice is diminished by these barriers is mandatory. If the NWFC concerns and opinions is not expressed, her ideas and her view will be unheard by Western corporations. However, the NWFC's ideas and view may be the difference between the international global online growth or death of Western corporations. The later becomes the case if the NWFC decides to refocus her collectivistic approach of utilizing word-of-mouth (WOM) in expressing dissatisfactions and concerns to family and friends in her local environment in order to protect her people. The effort for Western corporations to take notice, pay attention, listen and validate the existence of the NWFC online can propel global consumer loyalty, increase international market shares, and promote online innovation. It is profoundly important that corporations learn to gain full support of the NWFC by (1) understanding her (which Chapters IV through V of this study addressed), (2) implementing strategies to combat platform difficulties, culture and language barriers that diminish the NWFC voice (addressed here in the conclusion), and (3) continuously strive to assist the NWFC (future research should address).

GLOBAL SENSITIVITY

As the NWFC interviews were concluded, each participant listed suggestions and ideas for possible solutions corporations can implement to assist her in expressing her concerns to Western corporations and to ease the process of her future complaints. The listed solutions included: Western corporations' personnel should be more culturally sensitive, be quick to respond to global distance and platform cost (phone and CMC connection cost), patience in explaining procedures and validation of their concerns. These solutions are essential. With proper communication training and emphasis on cultural and international relations, these solutions can be implemented. For example, if Western corporations' personnel were sensitive to the NWFC global connection fees formalities, such as cost of the platform (phone minutes/online connection) for the NWFC when she contacts Western corporations but is placed on hold or never emailed back, a significant decreased in cost during phone interactions or online communication can change and build the loyalty and positive perspective of the NWFC in communicating with Western corporations.

Twenty-four hour order taking and customer response capability, and a customer identification system (Quelch & Klein, 1996; Usunier & Lee, 2005) allows for 24-hour identity clarification which prompts Western corporations the ability to assist the NWFC quickly by phone and provide full customer response answers of detailed information by email. Most customers gain a sense of loyalty when they feel that they are being taking seriously and their problems are resolved without delay. This issue was emphasized by the NWFC interview participants. As the NWFC gives loyalty, she seeks it back from Western corporations. Taking quick steps, no more than a few minutes, to restore the NWFC's positive thoughts of the corporations will save the corporations' reputation. Being sensitive to the NWFC's global demands and displaying a caring attitude will not only project the NWFC voice, promote positive WOM and customer loyalty but it will also allow her to express her dissatisfaction, feel appreciated and cared for by Western corporations.

NEED TO BELONG: AMPLIFYING THE NWFC'S VOICE

Everyone wants to belong, be heard, and be recognized, and the NWFC is by nature a communicator (Kirkup, 2007). If Western corporations want to befriend the NWFC, they must make changes in international consumer communication interaction, approach and complaint resolution. Some of the NWFC interview participants emphasized that the corporations should train personnel on cultural sensitivity. Such cultural sensitivity issues as discrimination based on the NWFC accent or her lack of proper English text, when emailing Western corporations, which she feels may prompts a recognition that she is foreign and thus is not provided with as much care as a Western female consumer or is not taken seriously, diminish her voice. In order to remove this perspective and damaging notion, mandatory efforts need to be implemented to cater to the NWFC as an accepted and valued consumer (Ardener, 1975) whose opinions and concerns matter. This study suggests that a dramatic change in recognizing the NWFC as a dominating global consumer must be acknowledged within Western corporations to include personnel with diverse international backgrounds and ethnicities to balance the consumer support initiative for global market.

Also, the use of the corporate customer CMC tool initiatives should be maximized to benefit the NWFC in expressing her concerns and opinions (Katz, 1959). Western CMC tools need to be efficient and timely in order to assist the NWFC. The lapse of time between the NWFC's complaint and the corporation's response should not be longer than 42-hours. Furthermore, there should be a response to every complaint made by a NWFC validating her concerns and promoting a sense of belonging (Maslow, 1987; Lim, 2010) in the Western consumer online sphere. Each response should be addressed to the individual NWFC consumer directly by the Western corporation's customer service personnel and not through an automated computer-generated response. It should be direct and unique to their concerns, opinions, or suggestions.

AN IDEAL CULTURAL BLEND

In assisting the NWFC, Western corporations must promote the need for an ideal cultural blend (See Figure 6.1 and Figure 6.2). Western corporation websites can cater to other languages and have more language options to communicate with the NWFC. This will fortify the connection between the Western corporations and the NWFC, and provide better clarification on product and item description which will allow the NWFC to have confidence in her online purchases and address concerns through her native language. In addition, this will promote the Western product trust factor that concerned many of the NWFC interview participants.

Western corporations should implement CMC platform methods that will provide the NWFC the ability to interact with their corporation personnel by installing online customer service video chat tools similar to Google Hangouts, Facebook chat, Skype. This will cater to the NWFC high-context culture norms and create a type of in-person environment on the virtual sphere. Furthermore, in order to resolve the NWFC lack of connection with Western corporations, there is a need to remove cultural restraints by accepting cultural limitation barriers (such as CMC hardtop and laptop communication tools) and creating platforms such as mobile text messaging which the NWFC is familiar with and uses daily to connect with family and friends. This will allow her to have a sense of connection with the Western corporations and also feel connected and valued.

These CMC tools and method implementations will (1) help the NWFC feel a sense of belonging and provide a better experience using Western corporations' CMC tools, which will encourage her to engage in online

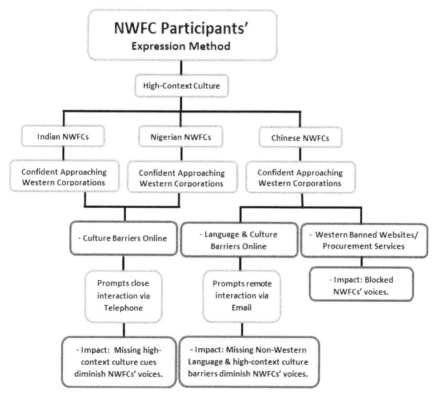

Figure 6.1. NWFC Interviewed Participants' Current Expression Method
Created by Chizoma C. Nosiri

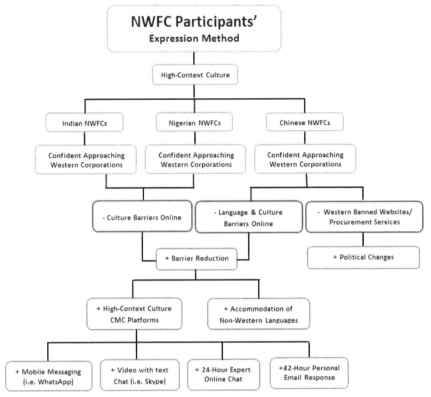

Figure 6.2.   NWFC Participants' Expression Method w/ Western Corp. Reform
Created by Chizoma C. Nosiri

shopping further while retaining her cultural norms; (2) amplify and cultivate the voice of the NWFC and give her the desire to voice her concerns,
opinions and innovative ideas to create ideal shopping experience both with
Western corporations and local native businesses; and (3) provide a massive
expansion of Western corporations' positive growth in the global sphere
while promoting the voice of the global female consumer.

LIMITATIONS TO STUDY

This study, as with any other study, has some limitations. It should be emphasized that the results of the NWFC participant interviews presented here
are intended to be indicative rather than statistically significant across the
general user population, unlike a Likert 5-point scale survey utilized in surveying populations. Although qualitative studies cannot be generalized, the

findings allows for a glimpse into the world of the NWFC, whose population is unknown. In addition, actions to generalize the NWFC restrict her cultural norms (high-context culture) to express her concerns in-person. In addition, quantitative research primary European elements of surveying, such as the Institutional Review Board (IRB) consent forms restrict the desire of the NWFC to complete the survey. Moreover, the English barriers of the consent form also blocks understanding of questionnaire surveys and further disengages the NWFC from completing questionnaire surveys or completing them accurately. Furthermore, CMC connectivity cost, the trust of CMC tools, and its unfamiliarity to the NWFC confounds the problem restricting her from completing questionnaire surveys. In light of these limitations, the most accurate and comfortable manner in which to allow the NWFC to respond accurately to the current study questions was to interview her through her preferred communication tool (i.e. video chat, mobile messaging, telephone, and email).

The NWFC interview participants who were interviewed for this study were between the ages of 23 and 54, and each interviewee's answers and opinions were strictly their own and cannot be used to generalize other NWFCs. Furthermore, time constraint impacted the findings of non-random sampling (snow-ball sampling) of various age groups of the NWFCs. In addition, due to the limited size of the interviewed individuals, understanding perspectives and views that impacted the behavior and actions of the NWFC interview participants may be limited. Thus, time limitations played a factor in the determination of the qualitative results.

This study of the NWFC deals with self-confidence (efficacy and ability), cultural and language barriers in the realm of Western online consumership for women who were born, raised and live in China, Nigeria, and India. Other areas of self-confidence, (i.e. family structure power or group separation issues) in the NWFC's life was not discussed. Only the online Western consumership role of the NWFC was explored. The study is restricted in analyzing, evaluating, and understanding the role that self-confidence, cultural and language barriers plays in the NWFC's life. Therefore, the generalization of the findings is limited since other NWFCs within this age group, with diverse background upbringings and different online Western consumer experiences might view their perceptions of self-confidence, culture and language barriers during their complaint situations differently.

RECOMMENDATIONS AND CONCLUSION

The recommendations provided in this study can serve as a measure to amplify the NWFC's voice in expressing her concerns to Western corporations and help foster stronger international communications and positive interpersonal relations for future communication between the NWFC and Western corporations. These recommendations also serve as a measure to improve global consumers' customer service experience, which will assist in blending the NWFC's culture with Western corporation's culture.

This research has revealed a flaw and missing component of the "mute" assumptions that is prevalent in the scholarship and framing of The Mute Group Theory created in 1975 by Edwin and Shirley Ardener. The assumed "muteness" of the NWFC and in many cases in other groups who are also considered "mute" are not strictly "muteness" in the terms that The Mute Theory expresses. The Mute Group theory focuses on how marginalized groups are muted (silenced and dominated) and excluded via the use of language. However, the theory does not include those who are muted by nature or nurture. While some individuals may be muted by social domination other individuals may be mute because they are introverts (or have levels of introvert personality traits), or mute by cultural upbringing. This mute nature or upbringing can then cater to being easily dominated since these individuals are prone to communication less verbally or rather not engage in conflict or lack assertiveness. Muteness should not be strictly observed or applied to minority groups but also inclusive of individuals who are mute from natureor nurture since they too can be oppressed and dominated. In addition, an individual can be "muted" because they are in a marginalized group and mute (nature/personally or nurture/culture). This finding is crucial since 30–50 percent of the world population is introverts (Myers et al., 1998; Feiler & Kleinbaum, 2015; Palmer, 2018) and are prone to being mute by nature or nurture.

It is crucial that the NWFC understands her significant role as a global consumer and how her voice and actions impacts the view of her, creates a negative discourse and prevents further recognition of her concerns. It is mandatory that the NWFC gains insight to strengthen and amplify her voice in the global sphere and continue to cultivate proactive behaviors to re-route the discourses of "muteness" that mischaracterized her. Her understanding and acknowledgement of the barriers that diminish her voice will allow her to cultivate ways in which she can eliminate the barriers. Since this current study has established the cultural and language barriers that diminish the voice of the NWFC, it is paramount that Western corporations note the NWFC's struggles and the barriers that diminish her voice. Empathizing with her will foster creations of virtual venues that cater to the NWFC and promote a sense of belonging for her. Western corporations must take initiative to amplify her voice and collaborate with her in reaching a cultural blend in order to build a truly global online sphere.

By applying theories and methods from non-traditional, organizational, conflict and communication areas, the present study provides a natural start-

ing point for future research of the NWFC and Western corporation relationship and complaint expression behavior. First, previous research in online
consumership has largely ignored the NWFC's perspective, global consumer
confidence, Western conflict and complaint behavior. No study has addressed
the assumed discourse of "muteness" associated with the NWFC virtual existence and a vast range of consumership issues are waiting to be studied on
this group. Second, exploring the NWFC present study in other Non-Western
locations (Japan, Ghana, and Pakistan) or focusing on particular generations
(ages 40 to 60 or ages 18 to 30), conducting in-depth interviews will provide
insight on the perspective of other NWFC individuals.

While this current qualitative study found correlation between the themes
discussed, it cannot clearly present a factual cause and effect relationship
to the barriers of culture and language and impact on the NWFC's communication behavior and action in interacting with Western corporations. The
themes discussed in this study may work together or alone. It depends on
the particular NWFC and her unique experiences. Furthermore, with cultural
sensitivity employed (i.e. video chat) and lengthy time structure provided a
quantitative research can be implemented in a manner to generalize findings
on similar areas of inquiry addressed by this current study.

The research paradigm used in the present study may be applied in future
research to investigate other virtual international gender context. Future
research should examine and elaborate on the perspective of the NWFC's
online consumerism behavior when engaging in conflict with Western corporations verses Non-Western corporations not local to her. Such a study
may give more insight to the NWFC's perspective on her view on Western
corporations and comparison of Western corporations to other foreign online
corporations. Another study can explore the difference between the NWFC's
confidence and conflict in family/friend situations compared to online consumer situations and the variables that constitute these differences. This study
could provide a clear understanding of how the NWFC behaves outside of the
virtual consumer environment and note distinguished cultural characteristics
that she embraces in the virtual consumer environment. Furthermore, a study
on social media platforms can be explored, understanding the perspective of
the NWFC in regards to Western social media platforms (Facebook, Twitter,
etc.) and Non-Western social media platforms such as the mobile messaging
applications (Wei Xin, aka QQ, or WhatsApp, or WeChat). Such a study will
give insight to how the global international community communicates and
provides ways in which Western corporations can accommodate the NWFC.

Appendix A

Examples of Online Non-Western Individuals' Complaints

INDIA

Raja of New Delhi, Other on May 7, 2014
Amazon Order
Satisfaction Rating1/5

"I ordered on 2nd May 2014 (for which I had paid instantly through online) and it was conveyed that it should reach with 5th May, 2014 to me. But after elapsing the next 48 hrs, I am still waiting for my stuff to come. Once contacted to the customer service operator I surprised to know that if the courier is unable to deliver the stuff and return back to Amazon, then only they can issue a refund only after getting their stuff back to them. So if the courier doesn't send it back to them in that case my refund will be all at sea!!!!!! So friends please think twice before making any order to Amazon as my experience was just too bad."

Retrieved on http://www.consumeraffairs.com/online/amazon.html

DIVYA of New Delhi, Other on April 13, 2014
Satisfaction Rating1/5

"I bought Sony 40EX520 on 12 Apr 12. After 20 months, one day there were horizontal lines on the screen. After reporting to Sony, they said that panel needs replacement and the estimated cost is Rs 22,000. The reason for failure given after 40 days pursuing the matter is "Natural failure may happen in a product in course of time and this is the reason why we offer 1 year of free service to our customers."

"I am surprised that a product like Sony which is priced at around 20% more than other, can say like that and it is accepted!! Also, I have seen on the net that there are so many complaints regarding this model and most of the failures happen after around 2 years of purchase, by which the warranty period is over. There seems to be manufacturing defect with few pieces but Sony is not bothered to analyse or deal with it. It is a shame! So, now I plan to take help of consumer court."

Retrieved on: http://www.consumeraffairs.com/home_electronics/sony_tv.html

CHINA

R of Hong Kong, Other on July 8, 2013
Satisfaction Rating1/5

"I have had two experiences with this company. The first was an urgent request for assistance on an anticipated crisis that fortunately, failed to materialize. I received no response, however, from CheapOair. Having failed to learn from my first experience, on a second airline booking, I needed to change the return date. The airline told me I could not change because CheapOair had placed a two-week restriction on the reservation. I found no such stipulation on the terms of service on my e-ticket. CheapOair failed to respond either to the airline's request or to my request for assistance/information."

"From my experience, it is plain that this company and or its staff are either lazy, incompetent and have no intention to provide customer service or simply are in bad faith. Stay away from CheapOair. By its conduct, it demonstrates that once it has your money, it has no further interest in you and is so worthless that it's prepared by that conduct to guarantee you will never want to do business with them again . . . I do not know whether these low fare entities function like bulk buyers of telephone services but I do intend to contact the airline sales departments involved to inform them of my experience with CheapOair in the hope that airlines have some regard for that character of the companies offering seats on their aircraft."

Retrieved on: http://www.consumeraffairs.com/travel/cheapoair.html?page=7

Sky of Hong kong, other on Jan. 9, 2012
Satisfaction Rating1/5

I got rejected for a personal loan and was told to see my credit report from TransUnion. TransUnion were the only credit reference agency in Hong Kong. I found not only did they put my gender wrong, they said I owed money to a supplementary credit card I had when I was 16 (should be under my parents). When they finally did "change" it (they only deleted it), they failed to alert other banks that the error was made by them.

Retrieved on: http://www.consumeraffairs.com/privacy/transunion.html?page=4

NIGERIA

komnavi of Lagos, other on Jan. 21, 2014
Satisfaction Rating1/5

"I bought a 2005 dodge grand caravan sxt, v6, 3.8cyl and shipped it to Lagos, Nigeria. Suddenly about 18 months ago, the engine began to run rough and the malfunction light came up. The fuel consumption is extremely high. The OBD machine read code po 202. We replaced the no 2 injector and the ECU (remanufactured and programmed). The cylinder head was also opened and all the valves ok. Still the problem persists. The car will not accelerate beyond 40 mph. At this point it jerks and and back thrusts. There is strong forward resistance at this speed. Can anybody please help me with suggestion that will solve this problem. I am here in Lagos very far from Chrysler."

Retrieved on: http://www.consumeraffairs.com/automotive/dodge_caravan.html

Sethuraman of Portharcourt, Other on July 9, 2010

"I am the Finance Manager of [company]. I have been sending my salary thru on line with Citibank Nigeria, Port Harcourt branch to India to my account number in SBI city branch in Coimbatore, South India. I have instructed the bank to remit the funds to my account number at SBI Coimbatore Branch at Swift code. But my funds are remitted by Citibank New York to SBI New York at their Swift code and then SBI New York is sending my funds after deducting $30 for every transaction. I fail to understand why SBI New York sends the funds to SBI New York while the instruction is to send to SBI India Coimbatore Branch. This has been going on since July 2009 and I am deducted US dollars from SBI New York. I have my other colleagues who send to SBI India in other cities and it reaches direct without going thru SBI New York and they get their salary in full. The problem must be with Citibank New York who has not updated the swift codes of SBI India, all branches especially their swift network is not updated with my ranch code number."

"Citibank Nigeria is not taking action to refund my money as the mistake is on Citibank New York who did not update the SBI Bank Swift codes for all branches in India. I am entitled to be compensated by Citibank New York for their mistake and they should update the SBI India all BIC codes in their network system so that I will get my salary in full in my bank account in India, Coimbatore SBI Branch like all other staff. I expect someone to help me solve my problems. Since July I am losing $30 per transaction. I have written SBI India, Citibank Nigeria and many other officers. But up to now no one has solved my problem. I am forced to change my bank account to another bank in India. I have been maintaining my account in SBI India since 1985 and changing my bank account to a new bank will create many inconveniences to me and my family in India."

Retrieved on: http://www.consumeraffairs.com/finance/citibank.htm?page=8

Appendix B

Non-Western Female Consumer Interview Questions

CONFIDENCE AND CONTACTING
WESTERN CORPORATIONS

Do you contact Western companies if you have a problem or a concern with their service or need to return a product?

Do you feel like you are confidence enough to call and speak up?

What is your confidence level when you express your concerns to Western companies'? If you could rate your confidence 1–10, 10 being the highest, what would it be?

What is your confidence level when you express your concerns to Western companies' personnel online?

What is your confidence level when you express your concerns on social media sites?

What is your confidence level when you express your concerns to local native businesses' personnel in your country?

What is your confidence level when you express your concerns to local native businesses' personnel in your country online?

What does self-esteem mean? How do you rate your self-esteem from 1–10 and why?

What does confidence mean? Do you think you have a low self-confidence or high confidence?

How would you rate your self-confidence level from 1–10 and why?

What is your confidence level when you talk to friends and family about your dissatisfactionwith Western companies?

Do you think your confidence impacts your decision to express your concerns to unsatisfying Western companies?

Are you confident with talking to Western companies if you had a problem?
If you do not express your concerns to Western companies in any way, why
don't you like to express your concerns to Western companies?

CONFLICT AND NOT BEING HEARD/UNDERSTOOD

How do you react to conflict?
Is it difficult to shop online with Western companies?
Have you had any experience where you felt that you had a concern about a
product or services or felt that you were mistreated, disrespect, or treated
unfairly by a Western company (online or in person)? If so did you contact
the Western company? How did you contact them?
If you did not contact them what was your reason?
If you had any experience where you felt that you had a concern about a
product or services, or felt that you were mistreated, disrespect, or treated
unfairly by a Western company (online) how would you contact them?
Have you had any experience where you felt that you were mistreated, disrespect, or treated unfairly by a local native business in your country, if so
what happened?
If you did not contact them what was your reason?
Did you contact the company, if so how and what happened?
Would you rather not discuss a concern or express yourself in order to avoid
conflict?
What are some ways you avoid conflict with a Western company when you
are dissatisfied with their services or their products? Please explain.
Have you ever been mistreated, disrespected, or treated unfairly online?
How you ever been treated unfairly or badly by a Western company? Please
explain Have you been mistreated or disrespected, while you were expressing your concern to a Western company?
Do you think your experience of being treated badly when you expressed
your concern has diminished your voice in speaking up when you are dissatisfied with a Western company online?
Do you feel like your opinion or concerns do not matter to local native businesses you have received dissatisfactory service from? Please explain.
Do you feel like your opinion or concerns do not matter to Western companies you have received dissatisfactory service from? Please explain.
What do you think will allow you to feel like you can express your concerns
to Western companies online?

NATURE VERSUS NURTURE

Do you think you are shy or timid? If so why?

WESTERN INTIMIDATION

Why don't you shop online often?
Do you feel intimidated by Western companies' personnel? Please explain.
Do you feel like Westerners are better than you? Please explain.
Do you feel like your opinion does not matter to Western companies? Please explain.
Do you find it easy to express your concern to Western companies' male personnel or Western companies' female personnel? Please explain?
Would you rather not express your concerns to Western companies' male personnel, but to local native businesses' male personnel? Please explain.
Are you intimidated by Western companies' computer tools? Please explain.
Are you intimidated by the personnel who read your complaint may be white (White males or White females)? Please explain?

COMPUTER-MEDIATED-COMMUNICATION
AND DEPENDENCY

How do you feel about computers?
How do you feel about Western companies' help tools online?
Do you find it difficult to approach a Western company's personnel through their online tool, if so why?
Are you unfamiliar with the online world and would rather not deal with it? Please explain?
Do you feel like the online world is hard for you to understand or different and hard to work with? Please explain.
Have you expressed your concerns to a Western company through their on-line consumer tools?
If so what tool did you use to express your concern?
Do you feel like you have to depend on others when you are trying to learn the online system? If so please explain?
Do you feel like because you don't know the online system or the computer very well that is the reason you do not express your concerns to Western companies?

Do you feel like the Western companies' tools are too difficult to use? Please explain?

Do you use email to contact Western companies when you have a concern? Please explain.

How do you feel about expressing your concern by email to Western companies?

When you received bad service or a bad product did you find another way of expressing your concern to the Western company? If so what did you do?

CULTURE

What is the best way for you to express your concerns about a company's bad service or product?

If you have a concern with a Western company's product/service who do you talk with in your local country and why?

How do you talk about concerns in your local culture?

Do you feel that someone who is expressing concern about bad service from a company or a bad product is complaining or just expressing their concern? What does complaining mean to you?

If you were to state your concern to a Western company personnel online about their service or their product, what do you think they will think about you?

Do you feel like you are an outsider and think different from Western companies' personnel? If yes, explain. If no, explain.

Do you feel like the Western culture and your culture are different so you cannot express yourself properly to Western companies' personnel? Please explain.

Do you feel you are disadvantaged in expressing your concern with Western companies that failed to satisfy your need as a customer because you are a female? If so why?

Do you feel you are disadvantage in expressing your concern with Western companies that failed to satisfy your need as a customer because you are not a Non-Westerner? If so why?

Would you rather talk to other people about your experience than address Western companies online? If so why?

Whom do you express your concern to or where do you express your concern or find answers when you are dissatisfied with Western companies?

How would you describe your approach of expressing your concerns about bad service or a bad product?

Do you let others speak for you if it is a local native business in your country? If so why?

Do you let others speak for you if it is a Western company? If so why?

Are there other things or reasons attached to your lack of expression of concern to Western companies? Please explain.

LOCAL NATIVE BUSINESS

Do you find it difficult to express your concerns when you contact local native businesses? If so why?

Do you contact local native businesses if you have a problem or a concern with their service or need to return a product?

Is it more difficult to express your concerns to Western companies or local native businesses?

Please explain why?

LANGUAGE

Are you able to write English well?

Do you feel that English is a problem when expressing your concerns?

Do you believe that not knowing English well diminished your voice in expressing yourself to Western companies? Please explain?

Do you feel you are disadvantaged in expressing your concern with Western companies online that failed to satisfy your need as a customer because you do not write English well? If so, explain further.

SOCIAL MEDIA

How do you feel about social media (Facebook, Twitter, etc.)?

Which would you rather use to express your concern about a Western company, the Western company's online tool or social media (Facebook, Twitter, etc.)? Please explain.

Do you think the online social media approach to express your opinion is a more convenient way to address your concerns than having Western computer-mediated communication tools? Please explain.

Is it more difficult to express your concerns to Western company personnel or express your concern through social media, and why?

What social media tools have you used to express your concerns about a Western company's service or product? Please explain why you used the particular social media platform.

Do you feel that social media has allowed you to express your concerns more about Western products or services?

What social media sites have allowed you to express your concerns about Western products or services?

Do you look at social media websites to read other people's negative experiences about Western services or products?

Do you look at social media websites to empower you to speak to Western companies about their bad products or services?

Have you been encouraged by others to speak up to Western companies through social media websites?

WORD-OF-MOUTH

If you did not use the Western company's online consumer help desk or email form to state your concern, what do you think would help you use it more to state your opinion?

When you received bad service or a bad product from Western companies did you tell your family and friends about it? Please Explain.

When you received bad service or a bad product from local native business did you tell your friends and family about it? Please Explain.

What is the easiest way for you to express yourself when you feel dissatisfied with a Western company's service?

What is the easiest way for you to express yourself when you feel dissatisfied with a local native business' service?

Appendix C

Consent Form

Consent for Investigative Procedures
Howard University
Washington, DC 20059

Non-Western Female Consumer Interview

Researchers from Howard University School of Communications are conducting this study to learn about Chinese, Nigeria, and India women consumer strategies when expressing their concerns about Western services/products online with Western companies (Unites States companies). The study also seeks to gain insight on social media usage by Chinese, Nigeria, and India women in expressing their concerns about Western services/products.

1. Procedure in the Investigation

The interview with the researchers will last 15 to 30 minutes on your computer. During that time, you will be asked several questions related to your experiences about your communication with Western companies online. You are free not to give answers to questions that make you feel uncomfortable. You are also free to end the interview and withdraw from the study at any time. You will not be identified in any papers or articles published from this research—in other words, you have complete confidentiality in all information you provide to the researchers.

This Consent Form asks for your permission to interview you and to video tape-record your answers on to assure that we have a complete and accurate record of your responses. Again, you will be guaranteed anonymity in all published reports.

2. Explanation to the Participants

Your participation in this research is voluntary. All precautions will be taken to reduce risks and to provide for your care during your participation. You are free to withdraw your consent and discontinue participation in the interview at any time without affecting your relationship with Howard University. The Howard University Institutional Review Board will have access to the records of this project. Dr. Richard Wright the principal investigator, is supervising the research Should you have questions that you would prefer to discuss with someone other than the investigators on this project, you are free to contact Howard University Institutional Review Board.

3. Purpose, Risks, and Benefits

We recognize that you may feel hesitant to discuss your observations and views regarding Western services/products and online communication with Western personnel. We also recognize that you may feel vulnerable in some way should others find out you have been a participant in the study. We recognize these concerns and honor them by allowing you to withdraw participation at any point in the interview or to skip questions that make you uncomfortable. While participation in this study will not benefit you directly, it will contribute to greater knowledge about Non-Western female online consumers and how they interact with Western personnel when they have concerns about Western services/products. We promise to respect your privacy and will maintain your confidentiality during the course of this study and in any reports that emerge from it.

4. Participant's Consent

Part A. I have read the above description of the research project. Anything I did not understand was explained to me by the researcher and my questions were answered to my satisfaction. I agree to participate in the above referenced project. I acknowledge that I received a personal copy of this consent form.

Participant's printed name

Participant's signature

Date

Part B. Tape-recorded interview:

I agree to have my interview tape-recorded for the purpose of providing the researcher with a confidential, accurate record of my information.

5. Investigator's Assurance

I, the undersigned, have defined and fully explained the procedures involved in this investigation to the above participant.

Researcher's signature

Date

Definition of Terms

The following terms were used in this research:

NWFC: The Non-Western female consumer (also known as The Global Female consumer) who was born, raised, and lives outside of Western countries (i.e. United States of America, England, and Australia) but buys and receives Western products/services online. She was born, raised, lives in a collectivistic culture. In this study the Non-Western female that was evaluated and observed was born, raised, and lives in China, Nigeria, or India. (See: Purpose and Reasoning for Scope of Study, p. 32 for understanding of the selection of the three countries).

Western Corporation: Any organization, business, corporation, or company within the individualistic culture (i.e. United States of America, Canada, England, Australia).

Corp.: Western Corporations (i.e. United States of America, Canada, England, Australia).

Local Native Business: Businesses created, managed, and operated by individuals who are from and live in China, Nigeria, or India (or collectivistic countries).

In-Person: Face-to-face interaction with local native business personnel in Non-Western countries.

CMC: Computer-mediated communication.

Muted Female: Most Western observers' perspective of muteness based on a cultural understanding that one is mute or muted if she does not directly communicate with corporations or express her concern to Western corporations she is unsatisfied with. A muted female is also defined through the

Western lens as a dominated female. One who is oppressed and tends to be ignored.

Confidence: In this study, confidence refers to self-confidence as self-efficacy, achievability, and capability.

Confidence change: Changes in the Non-Western female's confidence to speak up and assert her concerns and opinions, how she sees herself in association with the Western online domain structure, corporate personnel of the West, and how they will respond to her.

Culture: Individualistic and collectivistic approach to communication which is based on upbringing in traditions, beliefs, customs, and ways of life of a particular society.

Virtual world: Existing and occurring on the Internet (online) or through computer-mediated communication.

References

Abdulraheem, S., & Oladipo, A. R. (2010). Trafficking in women and children: A hidden health and social problem in Nigeria. *International Journal of Sociology and Anthropology*, *2*(3), 034–039.

Agamba, J., & Keengwe, J. (2014, March). Enhancing Objectives Writing Practices of Higher Education Faculty. In *Society for Information Technology & Teacher Education International Conference* (Vol. 2014, No. 1, pp. 713–717).

Agarwal, B. (1997). "Bargaining" and Gender Relations: Within and Beyond the Household. *Feminist Economics*, 3(1), 1–51.

Agarwal, B. (2003). Gender and land rights revisited: exploring new prospects via the state, family and market. *Journal of Agrarian Change*, 3(1–2), 184–224.

Ahmed, S., & Jaidka, K. (2013). Protests against# delhigangrape on Twitter: Analyzing India's Arab Spring. *eJournal of eDemocracy and Open Government*, *5*(1), 28–58.

Aina, Olabisi. (1998). "The Silent Partners of the Women's Movement" In Obioma Nnaemeka (ed): *Sisterhood, Feminism and Power from Africa to the Diaspora* pp. 65–88. Trenton New Jersey: Africa World Press Inc.

Aiyar, S. S. A. (2012). "Hidden Benefits of the Brain Drain" *Cato Institute*. Retrieved on February 15, 2015 from http://www.cato.org/publications/commentary/hidden -benefits-brain-drain.

Albirini, A. (2008). The Internet in developing countries: a medium of economic, cultural and political domination. *International Journal of Education & Development using Information & Communication Technology*, *4*(1).

Alcoff, L. (1991). The problem of speaking for others. *Cultural critique*, 5–32.

Al-Mahmood, S. Z., & Banjo, S. (2013). "Deadly Collapse in Bangladesh" *The Wall Street Journal*. Retrieved on February 15, 2015 from http://online.wsj.com/news/articles/SB10001424127887324874204578441912031665482

al-Natour, M. (2012). The Role of Women in the Egyptian 25th January Revolution. *Journal of International Women's Studies*, *13*(5).

Ardener, E. (1975). *'The "Problem" revisited,'* in S. Ardener (ed), Perceiving Women, London: Halsted Press.

Ardener, S. (1978). Introduction: The nature of women in society. *Defining females*, 9–48.

Asher, J. (1987). Born to be shy. *Psychology Today*, 21(4), 56.

Ayyash-Abdo, H. (2001). Individualism and collectivism: The case of Lebanon. *Social Behavior and Personality: an international journal*, *29*(5), 503–518.

Babbie, E.R. (2005). *The Basics of Social Research*. London, UK: Thomson Wadsworth.

Balka, E. (1995). Women's access to online discussions about feminism. *St. Johns: Computer Professionals for Social Responsibility*. Retrieved on February 15, 2015 from: http://feminism.eserver.org/gender/cyberspace/feminist-use-of -cyberspace.txt.

Balka, E., & Smith, R. (Eds.). (2000). *Women work and computerization*. Boston: Kluwer Academic Publishers.

Band, W., & Petouhoff, N. L. (2009). Topic overview: Social CRM goes mainstream. *Future*.

Bandow, D. (2014). Who Can Save "Our Girls" and Nigeria? Only the Nigerian People, Not Washington. Retrieved on February 16, 2015 from: http://www .cato.org/publications/commentary/who-can-save-our-girls-nigeria-only-nigerian -people-not-washington.

Barrett, D. (2006). *Leadership Communication*. McGraw-Hill. p. 197. ISBN 978-0-07-291849-6.

Beebe, S., Ivy, D., & Beebe, S. (2012). *Communication Principles for a Lifetime*, 5th edition Loose Leaf. Pearson Education, Inc.

Bertaux, D. (1981). "From the Life-History Approach to the Transformation of Socilogical Practice," in: *Biography and Society: The Life History Approaches in the Social Sciences*, D. Bertaux (ed.). Beverly Hills, CA, USA: Sage Publications Ltd, pp. 29–45.

Bickerstaff, S. (1999). Shackles on the Giant: How the Federal Government Created Microsoft, Personal Computers, and the Internet. *Tex. L. Rev.*, *78*, 1.

Biggs, S. (2000). Global village or urban jungle: Culture, self-construal, and the Internet. In *Proceedings of the Media Ecology Association* (Vol. 1, p. 28).

Bogdan, R. C., & Biklen, S. K. (2007). *Qualitative research for education: An introduction to theory and methods* (5th ed.). Boston, MA: Pearson Education.

Bowers, C.A. (1998). "The paradox of technology: what's gained and lost?." *Thought & Action, Vol., 14, no.* 1, pp. 49–57.

Boyer, A. L., Comby, E., Flaminio, S., Le Lay, Y. F., & Cottet, M. (2018). The social dimensions of a river's environmental quality assessment. Ambio, 1–14.

Braidotti, R. (Ed.). (1994). *Women, the environment and sustainable development: towards a theoretical synthesis*. Zed Books.

Brizendine, L. (2006). *The female brain*. London: Bantam Press.

Brody, L. R., & Hall, J. A. (2000). *Gender, emotion, and expression*. In M. Lewis & J. M. Haviland-Jones (Eds.), Handbook of emotions (2d ed., pp. 338–349). New York: Guilford.

Brosnan, M., & Lee, W. (1998). A cross cultural comparison of gender differences in computer attitudes and anxiety: the UK and Hong Kong. *Computers in Human Behavior*, 14(4), 559–577.

Brueton, V. C., Stevenson, F., Vale, C. L., Stenning, S. P., Tierney, J. F., Harding, S., & Rait, G. (2014). Use of strategies to improve retention in primary care randomised trials: a qualitative study with in-depth interviews. *BMJ open*, 4(1), e003835.

Carroll, D. (2012). *United Breaks Guitars: The Power of One Voice in the Age of Social Media*, California: Hay House.

Catalyst. (2013). *Catalyst Quick Take: Buying Power*. New York: Catalyst. Retrieved on February 16, 2015 from: http://www.catalyst.org/knowledge/buying-power.

Chakrabarti, M., & Shamugam, K. (2013) 'Hit Before You Run, The Telegraph. Retrieved on February 16, 2015 from http://www.telegraphindia.com/1130308/jsp/atleisure/ story_16648447.jsp#.Ui2tmcirHSg.

Chen, G., Gully, S. M., & Eden, D. (2001). Validation of a new general self-efficacy scale. *Organizational research methods*, 4(1), 62–83.

Cluff, C. C. N. (2012). *The Non-Communicative Female Consumer: A Look at Conflict & Confidence* (Master's Thesis, Bowie State University).

Cooke-Jackson, A. F., Orbe, M. P., Ricks, J., & Crosby, R. A. (2014). Relational, Pleasure, and Fear-Associated Aspects of Condom Use for Disease Prevention: A Qualitative Study of High-Risk African American Men. *Qualitative Research Reports in Communication*, *14*(1), 62–68.

Consumer Affairs (2014). Consumer Affairs for Brands. Consumer Reviews and Complaints. Retrieved on February 16, 2015 from http://www.consumeraffairs .com.

Crystal, D. (2001). *Language and the Internet*. Cambridge University Press.

Colgan, J. (2010). *Diamonds are a girl's best friend*. Hachette Digital.

Cronin, C. (2014). Using case study research as a rigorous form of inquiry. *Nurse Researcher*, *21*(5), 19–27.

Dallal, E. G. (1998). *Some Aspects of Study Design*. Retrieved on February 16, 2015 from http://www.jerrydallal.com/lhsp/study.htm.

D'Argembeau, A., & Van Der Linden, N. (2008). Remembering pride and shame: self-enhancement and the phenomenology of autobiographical memory. *Memory*, 16, 538–546.

Davis, E. (2012). *It's A Girl!* [Documentary] United States: Shadowline Films.

Delanty, G. (2007). *"Modernity." Blackwell Encyclopedia of Sociology*, edited by George Ritzer. 11 Vols. Malden, Mass.: Blackwell Publishing.

Denzin, N. K., & Lincoln, Y. S. (Eds.). (2011). *The SAGE handbook of qualitative research*. Sage.

DeVito, Joseph (2010). *Principles and Practices of Effective Communication* (Loose-Leaf Package) Belmont, MA: Allyn & Bacon Publishers, ISBN: 9780558780371.

Dholakia, R. R., Dholakia, N., & Kshetri, N. (2004). Gender and Internet usage. *The Internet encyclopedia*.

Dillman D., Smyth J., & Christioan L. M. (2009). *Internet and Mixed-Mode Surveys. The Tailored Design Method*. John Wiley & Sons. New Jersey.

Dong, C., & Li, Y. (2007). Conflict resolution in Chinese family purchase decisions: The impact of changing female roles and marriage duration. *International Journal of Conflict Management*, 18(4), 308–324.

Dörnyei, Z., & Csizér, K. (2002). Some dynamics of language attitudes and motivation: Results of a longitudinal nationwide survey. *Applied Linguistics*, *23*(4), 421–462.

Durndell, A., & Haag, Z. (2002). Computer self-efficacy, computer anxiety, attitudes towards the Internet and reported experience with the Internet, by gender, in an East European sample. *Computers in human behavior*, *18*(5), 521–535.

Durndell, A., & Thomson, K. (1997). Gender and computing: a decade of change? *Computers and Education*, 28(1), 1–9.

Eagly, A. H., & Karau, S. J. (2002). Role congruity theory of prejudice toward female leaders. *Psychological Review*, 109, 573–598.

Eagly, A. H. (2005). Achieving relational authenticity in leadership: Does gender matter? *The Leadership Quarterly*, 16, 3, pp. 459–474.

Eaton, L., & Louw, J. (2000). Culture and self in South Africa: Individualism-collectivism predictions. *The Journal of Social Psychology*, 140(2), 210–217.

Embassy, U. S. (2014). US Military to Assist in Search for Missing Nigerian Girls.

Evans, K. (1995). *Barriers to participation of women in technological education and the role of distance education.* Occasional paper No.Ê 1. Vancouver: Commonwealth of Learning.

Ezumah, N. (2008). *Perception of Womanhood in Nigeria and the Challenge of Development.*

Fan, C. (2003). Rural-urban migration and gender division of labor in transitional China. *International Journal of Urban and Regional Research*, 27(1), 24–47.

Fels, A. (2004). Do Women Lack Ambition? *Harvard Business Review,* 82(4), pp.50–60.

Flick, U. (2014). *An introduction to qualitative research*. London: Sage.

Foucault, M. (1972). The discourse on language. *Truth: Engagements Across Philosophical Traditions*, 315–335.

Fraser, N. (2009). *Feminism, capitalism and the cunning of history*. New Left Review, 5, 97–117.

Freud, S. (1895). (Re-examined: 1966). "Project for a Scientific Psychology," *Standard Edition*, Vol. 1, Hogarth Press.

Freud, S. (1993). Observations on transference-love: Further recommendations on the technique of psycho-analysis III. *The Journal of psychotherapy practice and research*, 2(2), 171.

Frey, L. R., Boton, C. H., & Kreps, G.L. (2000). *Investigating Communication: An Introduction to Research Method.* New Jersey: Prentice Hall.

Fromm, E., & Funk, R. (2013). *The revision of psychoanalysis*. Open Road Media.

Fukuyama, Francis. (1999). *The Great Disruption*. New York: Touchstone.

Fusilier, M., Durlabhji, S., Cucchi, A., & Collins, M. (2005). A four-country investigation of factors facilitating student Internet use. *CyberPsychology & Behavior*, *8*(5), 454–464.

Gibbs, S. (1998). Women on the Web: a two-year journey in cyberspace. *The European Journal of Womens Studies*, 5, 253–261.

Gilpin, R. (2018). The challenge of global capitalism: The world economy in the 21st century. Princeton University Press.

Gilroy, P. (1993). *The black Atlantic: Modernity and double consciousness*. Harvard University Press.

Gjoka, M., Kurant, M., Butts, C. T., & Markopoulou, A. (2010). Walking in Facebook: A case study of unbiased sampling of osns. In *INFOCOM, 2010 Proceedings IEEE* (pp. 1–9).

Glaser, B.G., & Strauss, A.l. (1967). *The Discovery of Grounded Theory: Strategies for Qualitative Research*. New York, NY, USA: Aldine Publishing Company.

Goldhaber, A. S., & Nieto, M. M. (2010). Photon and graviton mass limits. *Reviews of Modern Physics*, *82*(1), 939.

Goldsmith, J. L., & Wu, T. (2006). *Who controls the Internet?: Illusions of a borderless world* (pp. 142–181). New York: Oxford University Press.

Gramsci, A. (1996). *Prison notebooks* (Vol. 2). J. A. Buttigieg (Ed.). Columbia University Press.

Gray, J. (1992). *Men are From Mars, Women are From Venus*. New York: Harper Collins.

Greenberg, J. G. (2002). Criminalizing dowry deaths: The Indian experience. *Am.UJ Gender Soc. Pol'y & L.*, *11*, 801.

Groves, R. M., Fowler, F. J., Couper, M.P., Lepkowski, J.M., Singer, E., & Tourangeau, R. (2013). *Survey Methodology*. New Jersey: John Wiley & Sons.

Guffey, M. E. (2009). *Essentials of Business Communication*. South-Western/Cengage Learning.

Hatch, J. A. (2002). *Doing qualitative research in education settings*. Albany, NY: State University of New York Press.

Hachten, W. A., & Scotton, J. F. (2006). *The world news prism: Global information in a satellite age*. Wiley-Blackwell.

Hall, J. A., & Mast, M. S. (2008). Are women always more interpersonally sensitive than men? *Impact of Goals and Content Domain. Personality and Social Psychology Bulletin*, 34, 144–155.

Hall, E. (1976). *Beyond Culture. Anchor Books.* ISBN 978-0385124744.

Handcock, M. S., & Gile, K. J. (2010). Modeling social networks from sampled data. *The Annals of Applied Statistics*, *4*(1), 5–25.

Harding, S. (1997). Multicultural and global feminist philosophies of science: resources and challenges. In Neeson, L. H., & Neeson, J. (Eds.), *Feminisms, Science and the Philosophy of Science*. Dordrecht: Kluwer Academic Publishers.

Harding, S. (1998). *Is science multicultural? Postcolonialisms, feminisms, and epistemologies*. USA: Indiana University Press.

Hargittai, E. (1999). Weaving the Western Web: explaining differences in Internet connectivity among OECD countries. *Telecommunications Policy*, *23*(10), 701–718.

Harper, G. (2004). *The joy of conflict resolution.* Gabriola Island, BC: New Society.

Harris, J. R. (2000). The outcome of parenting: What do we really know?. *Journal of Personality*, 68(3), 625–637.

Harris, R. (2013). "Northern Nigeria: The Illo Canceller and Borgu Mail" *Cameo*, Vol. 14, No. 3, Whole No. 90, October 2013, pp. 158–160.

Hartman, S. (2008). Venus in two acts. *small axe*, *12*(2), 1–14.

Hellsten, L. M., Preston, J. P., Prytula, M. P., & Jeancart, D. P. (2014). Exploring the Experiences of a Small Group of Saskatchewan Neophyte Aboriginal Teachers. *in education*, *19*(2).

Hofstede G. (2001). *Culture's consequences: comparing values, behaviors, institutions and organizations across nations.* Thousand Oaks, CA: Sage Publications.

Hollos, M., Larsen, U., Obono, O., & Whitehouse, B. (2009). The problem of infertility in high fertility populations: meanings, consequences and coping mechanisms in two Nigerian communities. *Social science & medicine*, 68(11), 2061–2068.

hooks, b. (1990). "Marginality as a Site of Resistance," in R. Ferguson et al. (eds), *Out There: Marginalization and Contemporary Cultures*. Cambridge, MA: MIT, pp. 241–243.

Houston, D. A. (2003). Can the Internet Promote Open Global Societies?. *Independent Review-Oakland-*, *7*(3), 353–370.

Houston, M., & Kramarae, C. (1991). Speaking from silence: Methods of silencing and of resistance. *Discourse & Society*, *2*(4), 387–399.

Huntington, S. P. (1996). The West unique, not universal. *Foreign Affairs*, 28–46.

Ishizuka, L (2013). 'Nonprofits respond to the Delhi gang-rape case,' The Christian Science Monitor. Retrieved on February 16, 2015 from http://www.csmonitor.com/World/Making-a-difference/Change-Agent/2013/0116/Nonprofits-respond-to-the-Delhi-gang-rape-case-video.

Ivankova, N. V. (2014). Implementing quality criteria in designing and conducting a sequential QUAN→ QUAL mixed methods study of student engagement with learning applied research methods online. *Journal of Mixed Methods Research*, *8*(1), 25–51.

Ivankova, N. V., & Plano Clark, V. L. (2018). Teaching mixed methods research: using a socio-ecological framework as a pedagogical approach for addressing the complexity of the field. International Journal of Social Research Methodology, 1–16.

Ives, P. (2004). *Language and hegemony in Gramsci*. London: Pluto Press.

Jackson, L. A., Ervin, K. S., Gardner, P. D., & Schmitt, N. (2001). Gender and the Internet: women communicating and men searching. *Sex Roles*, 44 (5–6), 363–379.

Johnson, R. B., & Christensen, L. B. (2004). *Educational research: Quantitative, qualitative, and mixed approaches.* Boston, MA: Allyn and Bacon.

Johnson, B., & Christensen, L. (2008). *Educational research: Quantitative, qualitative, and mixed approaches.* Sage.

Johnson, R. B., & Onwuegbuzie, A. (2006). *Mixed methods research: A research paradigm whose time has come.* Educational Researcher, 33(7), 14–26.

Jaggar, A. M. (1998). Globalizing feminist ethics. *Hypatia*, 13(2), 7–31.

Jensen, M. (2000). African Internet Status. *Association for Progressive Communications,* November.

Joiner, R., Gavin, J., Duffield, J., Brosnan, M., Crook, C., Durndell, A., & Lovatt, P. (2005). Gender, Internet identification, and Internet anxiety: Correlates of Internet use. *CyberPsychology & Behavior, 8*(4), 371–378.

Joo, J. E. (1999). Cultural issues of the Internet in classrooms. *British Journal of Educational Technology, 30*(3), 245–250.

Jordan, T. (1999). *Cyberpower: The culture and politics of cyberspace and the Internet.* Psychology Press.

Kaberry, Phyllis, M. (1952). "Women Of The Grass Fields A Study Of The Economic Position Of Women In Bamenda, British Cameroons" *Her Majesty's Stationery office,* London, United Kingdom.

Kanter, R. M. (2005). How leaders gain (and lose) confidence. *Leader to Leader, 2005*(35), 21–27.

Kaplan, R. M., & Saccuzzo, D. P. (2009). *Psychological testing: Principles, applications, and issues.* Belmont, CA: Wadsworth.

Kapoor, I. (2002). Capitalism, culture, agency: dependency versus postcolonial theory. *Third World Quarterly, 23*(4), 647–664.

Kearl, H. (2018). The Facts Behind the# metoo Movement: A National Study on Sexual Harassment and Assault (Executive Summary).

Kim, A. J. (2000). *Community building on the Web. The Peachpit guide to webtop publishing.* Berkeley, Calif: Peachpit Press.

Kohn, M. (2006). *Colonialism.* Stanford Encyclopedia of Philosophy. Retrieved on February 16, 2015 from http://stanford.library.usyd.edu.au/entries/colonialism.

Kovel, J. (2007). *The enemy of nature: The end of capitalism or the end of the world?.* Zed Books.

Kramarae, C. (1981). *Women and men speaking: Frameworks for analysis.* Rowley, Massachusetts: Newbury House Publishers.

Kumari, R. (1989). *Brides are not for burning: Dowry victims in India.* Sangam.

Kuruc, K. (2008). Fashion as communication: A semiotic analysis of fashion on 'Sex and the City.' *Semiotica, 2008*(171), 193–214.

Lalwani. A. K. (2009). The Distinct Influence of Cognitive Busyness and Need for Closure on Cultural Differences in Socially Desirable Responding. *Journal of Consumer Research*: 090114112719036 DOI: 10.1086/597214.

Land, P. (2014). Telic and paratelic, 122–127. *Reversal Theory: Applications and Development, 73*(74), 197.

Langmia, K., & Glass, A. (2014). Coping with Smart Phone 'Distractions' in a College Classroom. *Teaching Journalism and Mass Communication, 4*(1), 13–23.

Larraín, J. (2000). *"Identity and Modernity in Latin America."* Cambridge, UK: Polity; Malden, MA: Blackwell.

LeDoux, J. E. (2003). *Synaptic self: How our brains become who we are.* Penguin.

Leung, L., & Wei, R. (2000). More than just talk on the move: Uses and gratifications of the cellular phone. *Journalism and Mass Communication Quarterly, 77,* 308–320.

Leung, Louis (2013). "Generational Differences in Content Generation in Social Media: The Roles of the Gratifications Sought and of Narcissism." *Computers in Human Behavior* 29 (3): 997–1006.

Li, N., & Kirkup, G. (2007). Gender and cultural differences in Internet use: A study of China and the UK. *Computers & Education, 48*(2), 301–317.

Lindlof, T. R. & Taylor, B. C. (2011). *Qualitative Communication Research Methods*. (3rd edition) Thousand Oaks, CA: Sage Publications.

Linneman, T. J. (2010). *"Gender in Jeopardy!: Timid Intonations on a Television Game Show"* Paper presented at the annual meeting of the American Sociological Association Annual Meeting, Hilton Atlanta and Atlanta Marriott Marquis, Atlanta, GA.

Lim, K. (2010). *Internet control and anti-control: An examination of public deliberation through networked media on civil sovereignty in China* (Doctoral dissertation, State University of New York at Buffalo).

Liu-Rosenbaum, A. (2018). Weaving "Eroticism, Cosmology, and Politics" in Early Female Technopop: Three Discourses with the Informatics of Domination. Popular Music and Society, 41(1), 16–38.

Losh, E., Coleman, B., & Amel, V. U. (2013). Will the Revolution Be Tweeted? Mapping Complex Data Patterns from Sites of Protest. *Selected Papers of Internet Research, 3.*

Lugones, M. (1993) "On the Logic of Pluralist Feminism" in Claudia Card, ed., Feminist Ethics, *Laurence: University of Kansas Press.*

Machin, D., & Mayr, A. (2012). *How to Do Critical Discourse Analysis: A Mulimodal Introduction.* Thousand Oaks, CA: Sage Publications.

Maravelas, A. (2005). *How to reduce workplace conflict and stress.* Franklin Lakes, NJ: Career Press.

Massey, D. (2013). "Vocabulary of the economy." After neoliberalism? *The Kilburn Manifesto.* Retrieved on February 15, 2015 from http://www.lwbooks.co.uk/journals/soundings/pdfs/Vocabularies%20of%20the%20econo my.pdf.

Maurer, M. (1994). Computer anxiety correlates and what they tell us: a literature review. *Computers in Human Behavior*, 10(3), 369–376.

McIlroy, D., Bunting, B., Tierney, K., & Gordon, M. (2001). The relation of gender and Background experience to self-reported computing anxiety and cognitions. *Computers in Human Behavior*, 17(1), 21–33.

McKenzie-Mohr, S. (2011). Telling stories without the words: 'Tightrope talk' in women's accounts of coming to live well after rape or depression. *Feminism Psychology,* 21(1), 49–73.

McLuhan, M. (1960). *Explorations in communication.* Boston: Beacon Press.

McPhail, T. L. (2010). *Global communication: Theories, stakeholders, and trends.* John Wiley & Sons.

Merriam-Webster. "Domination." (2015). Retrieved February 16, 2015, from http://www.merriam-webster.com/dictionary/domination.

Merriam-Webster. "Hegemony." (2015). Retrieved February 16, 2015, from http://www.merriam-webster.com/dictionary/hegemony.

Maslow, A. (1987). *Maslow's Hierarchy of Needs.* Salenger Incorporated.

McEvoy, R., Ballini, L., Maltoni, S., O'Donnell, C. A., Mair, F. S., & MacFarlane, A. (2014). A qualitative systematic review of studies using the normalization process theory to research implementation processes. *Implementation Science*, 9(1), 2.

Miller, K. (2005). *Communication theories.* McGraw-Hill.

Moore, D., & McCabe, D. (1993). *Introduction to the practice of statistics.* New York: Freeman.

Myers, I. B., McCaulley, M. H., Quenk, N. L., & Hammer, A. L. (1998). MBTI manual: A guide to the development and use of the Myers-Briggs Type Indicator (Vol. 3). Palo Alto, CA: Consulting Psychologists Press.

Obradovich, J. D. (2009). *Influence of leadership and culture on financial performance: A case study in a troubled industry.* Dissertations, Capella University.

Odell, P. M., Korgen, K. O., & Schumacher, P., et al. (2000). Internet use among female and male college students. *CyberPsychology & Behavior,* 3(5), 855–862.

Okonofua, F. E., Ogbomwan, S. M., Alutu, A. N., Kufre, O., & Eghosa, A. (2004). Knowledge, attitudes and experiences of sex trafficking by young women in Benin City, South-South Nigeria. *Social Science & Medicine,* 59(6), 1315–1327.

Olu Pearce, T. (1999). She will not be listened to in public: perceptions among the Yoruba of infertility and childlessness in women. *Reproductive Health Matters,* 7(13), 69–79.

Onwuegbuzie, A. J., & Byers, V. T. (2014). An Exemplar for Combining the Collection, Analysis, and Interpretations of Verbal and Nonverbal Data in Qualitative Research. *International Journal of Education,* 6(1), p183–246.

Onwuegbuzie, A. J., Dickinson, W. B., Leech, N. L., & Zoran, A. G. (2007). *Toward more rigor in focus group research: A new framework for collecting and analyzing focus group data.* Paper presented at the annual meeting of the Southwest Educational Research Association, San Antonio, TX.

Oyewumi, O. (2002). Conceptualizing gender: the eurocentric foundations of feminist concepts and the challenge of African epistemologies. *Jenda: A Journal of Culture and African Women Studies,* 2(1), 1–9.

Oyserman, D., & Lee, S. W. (2008). Does culture influence what and how we think? Effects of priming individualism and collectivism. *Psychological Bulletin,* 134(2), 311.

Palmer, A. Echoes of acedia: introverts and perfectionists in the Church. HOLINESS VOLUME 4 (2018) ISSUE, 95.

Palmgreen, P., Wenner, L., & Rosengren, K. (1985). "Uses and gratifications research: The past ten years.." *Media gratifications research:* 1–37.

Pang, A., Hassan, N. B. B. A., & Chong, A. C. Y. (2014). Negotiating crisis in the social media environment: evolution of crises online, gaining credibility offline. *Corporate Communications: An International Journal,* 19(1), 7–7.

Parkes, C. M. (1988). Bereavement as a psychosocial transition: Processes of adaptation to change. *Journal of Social Issues,* 44, 53–65.

Pearce, T. O. (1999). She Will Not Be Listened to in Public: Perceptions among the Yoruba of Infertility and Childlessness in Women. *Reproductive Health Matters,* 69–79.

Pflug, J. (2009). Folk theories of happiness: A cross-cultural comparison of conceptions of happiness in Germany and South Africa. *Social Indicators Research,* 92(3), 551–563.

Powell, B., & Skarbek, D. (2006). Sweatshops and third world living standards: Are the jobs worth the sweat?. *Journal of Labor Research,* 27 (2), 263–274.

Quelch, J. A., & Klein, L. R. (1996). The Internet and international marketing. *Sloan Management Review*, 37(3).

Richins, L. M. (2009). Negative Word-of-Mouth by Dissatisfied Consumers: *A Pilot Study. Journal of Marketing*, 47, 1.

Robin, D. A. (2003). *Between East and West: The Moluccas and the Traffic in Spices Up to the Arrival of Europeans*. (August 2003). Diane Publishing Company.

Robson, C. (2011). *Real world research: a resource for users of social research methods in applied settings*. Chichester: Wiley.

Savicki, V., & Kelley, M. (2000). Computer mediated communication: gender and group composition. *CyberPsychology & Behavior*, 3(5), 817–833.

Schaarschmidt, M., & Kilian, T. (2014). Impediments to customer integration into the innovation process: A case study in the telecommunications industry. *European Management Journal*, 32(2), 350–361.

Scherbaum, C. A., Cohen-Charash, Y., & Kern, M. J. (2006). Measuring general self-efficacy A comparison of three measures using item response theory. *Educational and Psychological Measurement*, 66(6), 1047–1063.

Schonenberg H., Weber B., van Dongen B. F., & van der Aalst W. M. P. (2008). Supporting flexible processes through recommendations based on history. In: Dumas M., Reichert, M., & Shan, M. C. (eds.) *International Conference on Business Process Management* (BPM 2008), Vol. 5240 of Lecture Notes in Computer Science, pp 51–66, Springer-Verlag, Berlin.

Schwarzer, R. (2010). The General Self-Efficacy Scale. Retrieved on February 16, 2015 from http://userpage.fu-berlin.de/~health/engscal.htm.

Schwarzer, R., & Jerusalem, M. (1995). Generalized Self-Efficacy Scale. In Weinman, J. Wright, S., & Johnston, M. *Measures in health psychology: A user's portfolio. Causal and control beliefs* (pp. 35–37). Windsor, UK: NFER-NELSON.

Siegle, D. (2011). Quantitative and Qualitative Comparisons and the 'Paradign War.' Word Press.com. Retrieved on February 16, 2015 from http://lon03 .wordpress.com/2011/10/28/quantative-and-qualitative-comparisons-and-the -paradigm-war.

Silva, E. B. (2000). The cook, the cooker and the gendering of the kitchen. *The Sociological Review*, 48(4), 612–629.

Simon, S. J. (2000). The impact of culture and gender on web sites: an empirical study. *ACM SIGMIS Database*, 32(1), 18–37.

Smartt, N. (2017). Sexual Harassment In The Workplace In A# MeToo World.

Smith, A. N., Fischer, E., & Yongjian, C. (2012), "How does brand-related user-generated content differ across YouTube, Facebook and Twitter?" https://www .academia.edu/4780160/How_Does_Brand-related_User generated_Content_Differ _across_YouTube_Facebook_and_Twitter.

Solagberu, B. A., Balogun, R. A., Mustafa, I. A., Ibrahim, N. A., Oludara, M. A., Ajani, A. O., & Osuoji, R. I. (2014). Pedestrian Injuries in the most densely populated city in Nigeria—an epidemics calling for control. *Traffic injury prevention*, 100.

Solomon, M. (2011). *Consumer Behavior: Buying, Having, and Being*. Pearson/ Prentice Hall.

Spivak, Gayatri Chakravorty. (1988). "Can the Subaltern Speak?" in *Marxism and the Interpretation of Culture*. Eds. Cary Nelson and Lawrence Grossberg. Urbana, IL: University of Illinois Press, pp. 271–313.

Sreejesh, S., & Mohapatra, S. (2014). *Mixed Method Research Design: An Application in Consumer-Brand Relationships (CBR)*. Imprint: Springer.

Sudarkasa, N. (1996). *The Strength of Our Mothers: African & African American Women & Families: Essays and Speeches*. Trenton, NJ: Africa World Press.

Terranova, T. (2000). Free labor: Producing culture for the digital economy. *Social text*, *18*(2), 33–58.

Tipaldo, G. (2014). *L'analisi del contenuto e i mass media.* Bologna, IT: Il Mulino. pp. 29–30. ISBN 978-88-15-24832-9.

Todman, J. (2000). Gender differences in computer anxiety among university entrants since 1992. *Computers and Education*, 34, 27–35.

Tomlinson, S. (2014). *DailyMail.* 'Police officer held after two teenage sisters,14 and 15, are found hanging from a village mango tree after being gang-raped in another day of shame for India.' (Published, May 29, 2014). Retrieved on February 16, 2015 from http://www.dailymail.co.uk/news/article-2642922/Two-teenage-sisters -14-15-hanging-mango-tree-gang-raped-Indian-village.html#ixzz37OyeA0ho.

Toulmin, S. E. (1990). *Cosmopolis: The Hidden Agenda of Modernity*. New York: Free Press.

Trafimow, D. (2014). Considering Quantitative and Qualitative Issues Together. *Qualitative Research in Psychology*, *11*(1), 15–24.

Turkle, S. (1995). *Life on the Screen: Identity in the Age of the Internet*. New York: Simon & Schuster.

University of Chicago Press Journals. (2009). *Don't Flatter Yourself: Why SurveyResearch Can Be Flawed.* ScienceDaily. (Published, February 25, 2009). Retrieved on February 16, 2015 from www.sciencedaily.com/releases/2009/02/090223221448 .htm.

Usunier, J. C., & Lee, J. (2005). *Marketing across cultures*. Pearson Education.

Versendaal, J., van den Akker, M., Xing, X., & de Bevere, B. (2013). Procurement maturity and IT-alignment models: overview and a case study. *Electronic Markets*, *23*(4), 295–306.

Wall, C. J., & Gannon-Leary, P. (1999). A Sentence Made by Men Muted Group Theory Revisited. *European Journal of Women's Studies*, *6*(1), 21–29.

Ward, L., (2008). Female Faculty in Male Dominated Fields: Law, Medicine, and Engineering. *New Directions for Higher Education*, 143, pp. 63–72.

Warschauer, M. (2000). Language, identity, and the Internet. *Race in cyberspace*, 151–170.

Way, B. M., & Lieberman, M. D. (2010). Is there a genetic contribution to cultural differences? Collectivism, individualism and genetic markers of social sensitivity. *Social cognitive and affective neuroscience*, *5*(2–3), 203–211.

Wei, C., & Kolko, B. (2005). "Resistance to globalization: Language and Internet diffusion patterns in Uzbekistan." *New Review of Hypermedia and Multimedia*, Vol. 11, no. 2, pp. 205–220.

West, C. (1990). The new cultural politics of difference. *October*, 93–109.

West, R. L., & Lynn H. T. (2010). "Uses and Gratifications Theory." Introducing Communication Theory: Analysis and Application. Boston: McGraw-Hill, 392–401. Print.

Whitely, B. (1997). Gender differences in computer related attitudes and behaviour: a meta analysis. *Computers in Human Behavior*, 13(1), 1–22.

Williams, R. (1985). *Keywords: A vocabulary of culture and society*. Oxford University Press.

Willig, C. (2001). *Introducing qualitative research in psychology: adventures in theory and method.* Buckingham: Open University Press.

Willig, C. (2013). *Introducing qualitative research in psychology.* McGraw-Hill International.

Wilmot, W. W., & Hocker, J. L. (2007). *Interpersonal conflict* (7th ed.). Boston, MA: McGraw-Hill.

Winslow, E. V. (2010). *All Women Are Not The Same.* Pittsburgh, PA: RoseDog Books.

Wodak, R., & Mayer, M. (2009). *Methods of Critical Discourse Analysis.* Thousand Oaks, CA: Sage Publications.

Ye, J. (2005). Acculturative stress and use of the Internet among East Asian international students in the United States. *CyberPsychology & Behavior*, 8(2), 154–161.

Yin, R. K. (2003). *Case Study Research Design and Methods.* Thousand Oaks, California: Sage Publications.

Yin, R. K. (2014). *Case Study Research: Design and methods.* Sage Publications.

Zhang, S., van Doorn, J., & Leeflang, P. S. (2018). Face Concerns and Purchase Intentions: A Cross-Cultural Perspective. In *Advances in Global Marketing* (pp. 213–249). Springer, Cham.

Zimmermann, A. (2014). Feminism and gendercide: Pro-choice feminism and the elimination of unwanted girls. *Quadrant*, 58(4), 24.

Index

About the Author

Dr. Chizoma Nosiri has a Ph.D. in Communication, Culture and Media Studies, graduating summa cum laude, awarded Highest Distinction for her dissertation which focused on international women, cross-cultural and inter-cultural communication, confidence, conflict and consumership. She received a Master's degree in Organizational Communications, graduating summa cum laude, awarded Highest Distinction for her thesis which focused on Western women, confidence, conflict and consumership. Dr. Nosiri speaks, coaches, lectures and researches on communication, self-esteem, confidence, public speaking, culture, organizational change, intrapersonal and interpersonal communication, gender, consumerisim, international communication, organizational communication, conflict mediation and resolution. As a change agent, Dr. Nosiri works with corporations, organizations and individuals to change their communication processes. She has been featured on several radio and television shows as a communication confidence guru.